Third Edition · Volume I

A Practical Business Chinese Reader

基础实用商务汉语
（第3版）

关道雄（Daoxiong Guan） ◎编著

北京大学出版社
PEKING UNIVERSITY PRESS

图书在版编目(CIP)数据

基础实用商务汉语. 上册 / 关道雄编著. —3 版. —北京：北京大学出版社，2018.1
ISBN 978-7-301-29132-0

Ⅰ.①基… Ⅱ.①关… Ⅲ.①商务－汉语－对外汉语教学－教材 Ⅳ.①H195.4

中国版本图书馆CIP数据核字（2017）第 326024 号

书　　　名	基础实用商务汉语（第3版）上册 JICHU SHIYONG SHANGWU HANYU (DI-SAN BAN) SHANG CE
著作责任者	关道雄（Daoxiong Guan）　编著
责任编辑	孙　娴
标准书号	ISBN 978-7-301-29132-0
出版发行	北京大学出版社
地　　　址	北京市海淀区成府路 205 号　100871
网　　　址	http://www.pup.cn　　新浪微博：@北京大学出版社
电子信箱	zpup@pup.cn
电　　　话	邮购部 62752015　发行部 62750672　编辑部 62753374
印 刷 者	三河市博文印刷有限公司
经 销 者	新华书店
	787 毫米 × 1092 毫米　16 开本　14.5 印张　215 千字 2000 年 9 月第 1 版　2003 年 9 月第 2 版 2018 年 1 月第 3 版　2024 年 5 月第 3 次印刷
定　　　价	78.00 元

未经许可，不得以任何方式复制或抄袭本书之部分或全部内容。
版权所有，侵权必究
举报电话：010-62752024　电子信箱：fd@pup.pku.edu.cn
图书如有印装质量问题，请与出版部联系，电话：010-62756370

To our students whose love of Chinese encouraged us to complete this book.

第三版修订说明

《基础实用商务汉语》是一部以一般商务用途汉语（Chinese for General Business Purpose or CGBP）为学习内容的教材。它所服务的对象主要是已经学习了一年到一年半汉语课程、对基本的现代汉语语法结构已有所了解的汉语非母语的学习者。

本书第三版的修订工作主要涉及以下几个方面。

（一）将原有的十六课分为上下两册，可供两个学期使用。

体例上保持了"内容上既前后衔接又相对独立"和"前八课稍易，后八课较难"[1]的设计，但对原来全书各课的先后次序做了微调。教师也可以根据自己学生的具体情况，选择使用其中的一册。

（二）更新课文内容。

第三版每课的课文内容（即"对话"和"阅读短文"）均有程度不同的更新。其中《广告与促销》的课文完全重写；《招聘面试》和《工业园区》两课为新增，替换了原有的《文化异同》和《经济特区》两课。这样做的目的是为了使课文话题和内容能够更好地切合中国经济发展的现实情况以及实际商务活动中的典型场景，增加本教材的实用性。

（三）大幅更新全书每课的"练习与活动"。

第三版的"练习与活动"分为三大部分，即"词汇练习""句型练习"及"阅读、讨论和其他活动"。作者在设计、编写这些练习与活动时，融入了交际法、任务教学、合作学习等理念，同时也不排除使用一些比较传统的练习、活动方式。此次修订着重充实了"词汇练习"与"阅读、讨论和其他活动"两大部分的含量，增加（或改进）了多种不同类型的练习、任务和活动。另外，每课"练习与活动"的最后部分均新增了"快速复习"。"快速复习"以补充阅读的形式呈现。阅读内容实际是对本课对话或本课与前一课两课对话的整合、重写。阅读材料中尽可能不出现任何本课和本课以前各课没有出现过的生词。这样设计的目的是为了帮助学习者巩固已经学过的内容，同时提高教材中词汇的复现率。商务汉语教材词汇复现率一直是一个不容易解决的问题。《基础实用商务汉语》第三版在修订

---

1 见初版前言。

I

过程中对这一问题给予了更多的注意。作者一方面有意识地让一些商务词汇在前后课文中多次出现，另一方面通过新增加的"快速复习"以及其他各项练习与活动来提供多次操练这些商务汉语词汇的机会。这些做法在一定程度上确实提高了本教材词汇的复现率。

（四）增加听力材料。

除了原有的课文对话、阅读短文和生词录音以外，练习部分中的一些句型练习和每课的快速复习部分的短文也配了录音。所有录音材料均以 🎧 符号标出。

（五）新增了扫二维码查看课文英译和听录音的功能。

为了给使用者提供更多的方便，第三版新增了扫码听录音和查看课文英译的功能。每一课大标题旁均印有一个二维码，加注"听力材料"字样。扫描该码后可以看到这一课按编号排列的（即001、002）所有听力材料的完整录音目录。点击任意子目录，就可以在线收听录音材料。此外，每课对话和阅读短文前的二维码，加注"课文英译"字样。扫描该码后即可在线阅读相应的英译材料。使用者也可以从北京大学出版社网站的下载专区（http://www.pup.cn/dl/newsmore.cfm?sSnom=d203）下载相应的录音文件，从书后的"总附录"中查看所有课文英译。

（六）修订每课的附录。

本书第三版对所有的附录材料都做了更新、替换，尽可能使本教材的附录材料对教与学都有一些实际的用处。

《基础实用商务汉语》第三版总词汇表共列词汇1114个，句型总表共收句型142个。每课的课堂教学时间一般为5—6课时。建议教师根据实际的教学情况作出必要的调整。

《基础实用商务汉语》一书自2000年出版以来，收到海内外很多使用者的热心反馈。这些意见对于本书的修订无疑有莫大的助益。北京大学出版社一直对本书的编写、出版和修订给予充分的支持和帮助。第三版责编孙娴女士为修订提供了很多有益的建议。作者在此一并表示诚挚的感谢。

关道雄 dxguan@ucsb.edu
2017年5月于美国加州大学
圣塔芭芭拉分校
东亚语言文化研究系

Preface to the Third Edition

A Practical Business Chinese Reader is a language textbook that teaches Chinese for General Business Purpose (CGBP). It aims to serve those non-Chinese speakers who have completed one to one and a half year of Chinese courses at the college level, as well as having an understanding of most of the basic modern Chinese grammatical structures.

The changes to the third edition of this textbook mainly cover the following:

1) Dividing 16 lessons into 2 volumes.

It preserves the design that "the contents of the lessons may be seen in the chronological order of events or as sixteen individual stories" and "the first eight lessons are more basic while the latter eight lessons are more advanced by comparison".[1] Nevertheless, the order of lessons in this edition has been adjusted slightly. Teachers may choose one of the two volumes for teaching based on the practical need from students.

2) Updated lesson content.

Of the lessons, "Advertising and Sales Promotion" has been completely rewritten; "Job Interview" and "Industrial Park" are newly added lessons, replacing "Cultural Similarities and Differences" and "Special Economic Zones". The purpose of doing so is for the topics and contents of the lessons to better represent the current state of Chinese economic development and typical scenarios in practical business activities, contributing to the practical usability of this textbook.

3) Large scale changes to the "Exercises and Activities" in each chapter.

In the third edition, the "Exercises and Activities" are split into three categories: "Vocabulary Exercises", "Sentence Pattern Exercises", and "Reading, Discussion, and Other Activities". In designing and composing these exercises and activities, the author blends the communicative approach, task-based teaching, cooperative learning, etc., while also keeping usage of some more traditional methods of exercises and activities. This edition heavily expands on the contents of "Vocabulary Exercises" and "Reading, Discussion, and Other Activities", adding (or enhancing) many different types of exercises, tasks, and activities. In addition, "Quick Review" was added to the last part of "Exercises and Activities" in each lesson. "Quick Review" is presented in the form of supplementary reading. The reading material is a simple combination and rewrite of the dialogues in the current lesson, or the current lesson plus the previous lesson. There are almost no vocabulary words new to the lesson or previous lessons appearing in this reading material. The goal of this design is to help students strengthen their grasp of material already learned, as well as raising the word recurrence frequency in the text. Word recurrence frequency has always been

---

1   See the preface, First Edition.

a difficult problem in Business Chinese teaching materials. *A Practical Business Chinese Reader* pays more care to this issue in the Third Edition. The author deliberately repeats some business Chinese vocabulary words throughout the text, while also providing opportunities for students to practice these words many times through the "Quick Review" and other exercises and activities. These approaches have indeed increased the word recurrence frequency in this text.

4) Adding more listening materials.

In addition to the original audio recordings of the dialogues, reading passages, and vocabulary words, new audio recordings have been provided for some Sentence Pattern Exercises and the Quick Review passages in each lesson. All audio materials have been marked with the 🎧 symbol.

5) Added functionality of scannable QR code to access English translations of the lessons and audio recordings

To provide greater convenience for the user, the Third Edition has added scannable QR codes to access English translations of the lessons and audio recordings. The QR code next to the title of each chapter marked with "Audio Recordings" contains a complete list of all audio recordings for this chapter. After scanning the QR code, you can view the full list of contents for all audio materials (e.g., 001, 002) for each lesson. You can click the links to listen to the recordings. In addition, QR codes placed before Dialogues as well as Reading Passages of each lesson are marked with "English Translation". Scanning these codes will allow you to read the corresponding English translations online. Users can also download the audio recordings from the website of Peking University Press (http://www.pup.cn/dl/newsmore.cfm?sSnom=d203), and look up all English translations of the lessons from the General Appendix at the back of the book.

6) Editing the appendices to each lesson.

In the Third Edition, all appendices have been updated or replaced, enhancing the practical value of the appendix material to both teaching and learning.

In total, *A Practical Business Chinese Reader Third Edition* includes 1114 vocabulary words and 142 sentence patterns. Each lesson will need approximately 5 to 6 hours of instruction time. It is suggested that instructors make adjustments based on their own teaching circumstances.

Ever since *A Practical Business Chinese Reader* was published in 2000, I have received enthusiastic feedback from many users in China and abroad. These comments have been immensely beneficial to the editing and revision of this book. The Peking University Press has always been greatly supportive and helpful with the composition, publishing, and revision of this book. The editor for the Third Edition, Ms. Sun Xian, provided many beneficial suggestions. The author expresses sincere gratitude.

Daoxiong Guan (dxguan@ucsb.edu)
Department of East Asian Languages and Cultural Studies
University of California, Santa Barbara
May, 2017

第二版前言

《基础实用商务汉语》一书自 2000 年出版以来，先后为国内外一些学校选用作教材。其韩文版亦于 2002 年由韩国多乐园有限公司在首尔出版。此次修订再版，除了订正原稿中的错误并更换、补充了若干课文中的部分内容以外，主要对每课的练习作了大幅度的扩充和调整。修订后的词汇总表共收入生词 1040 个，句型总表共收入句型 154 个。

需要说明的是，本书的原作者之一遇笑容教授因为出任加州大学海外学习项目驻华中心主任，此次未能参与修订工作。但是本书得以成稿问世却是与她的长期关心、支持与参与分不开的。北京大学出版社的徐刚先生和郭力女士从本书的撰写到修订出力甚多，在此一并表示感谢。

关道雄
2003 年 3 月于美国加州大学
圣塔芭芭拉分校
东亚语言文化研究系

Preface to the Second Edition

Since it was first published in 2000, *A Practical Business Chinese Reader* has been adopted as a textbook by schools in China and overseas. The Korean edition (*Ok! Business Chinese*) was published by Darakwon Inc. at Seoul in 2002. This revised edition has corrected some mistakes and partially replaced or replenished content in several lessons. However, the majority of the revision was made to the exercises in each lesson. Almost all the exercises have been rewritten or redesigned. As a result, the number of the exercises in this book has increased by as many as 3-4 times. There are only slight changes in vocabulary and sentence patterns. A total of 1040 new words and 154 sentences patterns has been introduced in the revised edition.

It was very unfortunate that Professor Hsiao-Jung Yu, the co-author of the original edition of this book, could not work on the new version of the book this time. She was appointed as director of the UC EAP (University of California Education Abroad Program) Study Center at Beijing last year and has committed herself completely into this immense responsibility. There is no doubt that it would have been impossible for me to complete this book from the very beginning without her support, concern, and contribution. Many thanks also go to Mr. Xu Gang and Ms. Guo Li at Peking University Press. Their continuous support and help have made the revision successful.

Daoxiong Guan
Department of East Asian Languages and Cultural Studies
University of California, Santa Barbara
March, 2003

初版前言

近年来，商务汉语在海外汉语教学中逐渐引起了相当的注意。在美国，目前已经有不少大学相继开设了商务汉语课程。一些大学甚至正在计划、酝酿开设层次不同、训练重点不同的系列商务汉语课。显然，商务汉语正开始成为对外汉语教学中的新热点。

商务汉语课的出现无疑与中国经济的迅速发展有着密切的关系。可以肯定地说，只要中国经济继续保持良好的发展趋势，商务汉语课的发展将是非常有潜力的。但是，作为一门新课程或者说新领域，商务汉语面临着众多急需解决的问题。其中，编写出版适合对外汉语教学所使用的商务汉语课教材的任务尤为迫切。这就是我们编写《基础实用商务汉语》的起因。

《基础实用商务汉语》一书的主要适用对象定位为至少已经学习了一年到一年半汉语、对主要的现代汉语语法结构已有所了解的学生。其已经掌握的词汇量应当在一千字左右，即大致相当于《汉语水平词汇与汉字等级大纲》中甲级词的水准。在编写体例与架构上，《基础实用商务汉语》一书共分为十六课，以一个美国商务代表团访问中国为线索，依次介绍了商务谈判的各项主要环节和其他相关的商务、社交活动。内容上既前后衔接又相对独立，以便任课教师根据需要调整自己的课程教学安排。就难易程度而言，前八课稍易，后八课较难。每课包括：

1. 主题对话；

2. 阅读短文；

3. 词汇和句型；

4. 练习和活动；

5. 附录。

全书最后编有总附录，包括全部课文的英译、词汇总表、句型总表、重要网址、中国地图和主要参考书目。全书共计列出生词1010个，句型152个。通过这本课本的学习，学生可望达到中级或中级以上的汉语水平。

把本书设计在上述的汉语水平层次上是基于这样的考虑。我们认为，商务汉语的学习应该在已经初步具有了一定的汉语语言能力的基础上进行。商务汉语课不需要也不应该在"商务"的名目之下再教授发音、识字或是最基本、最常用的汉语词汇和语法。如果要那样做的话，势必会模糊一般对外汉语课和商务汉语课的界限。商务汉语课应该是一门具有特定目标、特定内容的对外汉语语言课程。它所提供的是现代汉语中常用的商务词汇的知识以及与此相关的社会、文化知识，培养学生在汉语语言环境中进行商务活动所需要的语言交际技能。作为对外汉语课程中的一种，商务汉语与普通汉语课存在着密切的联系。但是商务汉语课的教学目的显然有别与普通汉语课。其教材与教法也应当具有自己的特色。换句话说，商务汉语课必须在其教学内容上提供普通汉语课无法提供的语言、文化知识，才能真正成为一门独立的、无法替代的课程。

基于上述的想法，我们在《基础实用商务汉语》一书的总体设计和具体编写中做了以下的尝试：

（一）注重培养学生在实际汉语语言环境中进行商务活动的语言能力。

能力语言教学法是近二三十年来在美国外语教学界一再讨论及推行的外语教学理论。能力语言教学法强调培养外语学习者实际的语言交流能力，把从书本上学到的语言知识及时地（即时地）运用在真实的生活情境之中。为了在商务汉语课中达到这一目的，《基础实用商务汉语》的课文选题力求概括最具代表性、最有普遍意义的实际商务活动。课文对话的编写力求真实而生动、实用且不乏风趣，尽可能避免单调的或教科书式的语言。每一课的练习与活动的设计均旨在鼓励学生的主动参与。在帮助学生理解课文内容的同时，尽量利用多种形式，为学生提供在真实（或模拟真实）的语境中操练、使用该课词汇与句型的机会。每课的附录则结合课文的需要，提供相关的中文商业信函、文件、表格等实例，以期帮助学生熟悉实际商务活动中可能接触到的这类材料，取得学以致用的效果。

（二）重视相关文化背景知识的介绍。

将文化背景、风俗民情、社交礼仪乃至思维方式的介绍融入外语教学之中的文化、语言融合教学法也是近年来欧美语言教学界讨论的重点之一。这种教学理论的一个明显的好处就是使学习外语的人可以通过语言的学习来了解文化、通过了解文化来提高其外语水平。我们觉得商务汉语教学有必要与文化知识的介绍相结合。了解中国人的思想、行为模式以及在待人接物上的种种习惯，将有助于在实际商务活动中有效的沟通与交流，避免某些不必要的误会。基于这样的认识，《基础实用商务汉语》一书在每课的主题对话之外，又安排了一篇阅读短文。其内容是与该课主题对话相关的社会背景、文化背景信息。换言之，本书每一课的主题对话是以具体的商务活动设立单元，而每课的阅读短文则是以介绍文化背景设立单元。在文体上，前者是口语，后者是书面语。这样不但可以同时训练学生的会话和阅读能力，同时也增加了学生的学习兴趣。

（三）从商务汉语的角度出发，合理挑选课文词汇和句型。

在从事对外汉语教学的实践中，我们深深感到课本词汇的合理甄选和使用是非常值得重视的一个问题。编写一本汉语教材，应该仔细审慎地考虑它所准备使用的字、词和词组。在决定哪些字词应该介绍给学生、哪些应该列为必需掌握的生词的时候，编写者应该尽量避免主观性和随意性。对外汉语课本中词汇的取舍标准无疑应该建立在科学统计的基础上。商务汉语课本更不能例外。根据《汉语水平词汇与汉字等级大纲》的统计，对外汉语教学基础阶段的词汇量应当以3000词为界标。根据我们的分析，在这3000个词中，有可能被收入任何一本商务汉语词典的词大约在百分之一左右。因此，一本理想的商务汉语教材所提供的基本词汇，应当能够最直接地反映出其不同与一般汉语课本的特征。在《基础实用商务汉语》一书的编写中，我们决定以《汉语水平词汇与汉字等级大纲》的甲级词表为界线。甲级词表共收词1033个，都是现代汉语中使用频率最高的基本常用词，也是初学者在基础阶段应该首先掌握的词汇。这样一个词汇量正好符合我们为本书使用者设定的汉语水平起点。因此，凡是被收入甲级词表的词汇，在这本教材中均被编者视为学生已经掌握的词汇，不再列入生词部分。必须说明的是，由于我们还缺乏商务汉语词汇使用频率方面的统计资料，因此在选择这方面的词汇的时候，本书可能有不少考虑不周的地方。我们真诚地盼望读者提出批评和建议。

　　《基础实用商务汉语》一书的内容和体例由关道雄与遇笑容拟定。关道雄负责主题对话、阅读短文、生词表、句型表的编写以及全书的统稿，遇笑容负责每课练习与活动的设计和编写。课文的英文翻译由史香侬（Shannon Lee Du）承担。中国江西财经大学经济文化传播系的熊焰、陈秀平教授审读了本书的初稿，并且为本书的附录搜集、提供了一些有用的信息和原始材料。陈毓贤女士（Susan Chan Egan，原美国 Scudder, Stevens & Clark, Inc. 资深证券分析师）为书中涉及的专业词汇的英汉对译解决了不少难题。在此一表示衷心的感谢。我们还应该特别感谢审读本书的北京大学出版社的郭力女士和徐刚先生。因为他们的关心和帮助，本书才能够得以顺利出版。

　　本书的初稿曾在加州大学圣塔芭芭拉分校试用。这使我们有机会在实践中对这本教材做出修改。在此我们也想对我们的学生表示由衷的谢意。正是他们对汉语学习的强烈兴趣和热爱给了我们编写本书的动力。

关道雄、遇笑容
2000 年 5 月于加州大学
圣塔芭芭拉分校
东亚语言文化研究系

Preface to the First Edition

In recent years, Business Chinese has drawn increasing attention in the field of overseas Chinese teaching. In the United States, some universities are already offering Business Chinese courses. Others are even considering or planning to offer series of Business Chinese courses at different levels, each placing the emphasis on various aspects. Obviously, Business Chinese is becoming a popular new course in the field of teaching Chinese as a foreign language.

The popularity of Business Chinese is a by-product of China's economy, which has grown rapidly in the last decade. There is no doubt that Business Chinese has a tremendous potential as long as China's economy maintains this positive trend and continues growing. On the other hand, Business Chinese as a newborn course is facing a number of questions that have to be solved without delay. What is most urgent and crucial now is to compile textbooks that properly fit the needs of Business Chinese in the field of teaching Chinese as a foreign language. That was our intention in writing this textbook, A Practical Business Chinese Reader.

A Practical Business Chinese Reader is designed for those who have completed at least one year to one and a half years of Chinese study at the college level and have gained a good knowledge of basic grammar in modern Chinese as well as around a 1,000-word vocabulary in Chinese, equivalent to the beginning level in Guidelines of Chinese Proficiency and the Degree of Difficulty of Chinese Characters. We believe that Business Chinese should be taught beyond the beginning level. There is no need to teach pronunciation, character writing or beginning level vocabulary and grammar in a Business Chinese course. Although there are similarities and connections between Business Chinese and other Chinese language courses, the goal of Business Chinese certainly is different than other Chinese language courses, and so is its content. Business Chinese courses train students to develop their communication skills both in oral and written forms in order to conduct business in a Chinese language environment. The emphasis is placed on the usage of business terms in modern Chinese and on language proficiency in a business context as well as on business related social-cultural awareness.

By following the progress of an American business delegation in China, A Practical Business Chinese Reader has developed sixteen lessons in all to introduce some typical business activities and business related social events in the Chinese business world. The contents of the lessons may be seen in the chronological order of events or as sixteen individual stories so that instructors may adjust their teaching plans according to their own needs. In terms of difficulty, the first eight lessons are more basic while the latter eight lessons are more advanced by comparison. However, these sixteen lessons, should they all be used, are sufficient for one semester or two quarters. Each of the sixteen lessons in the book contains the following sections:

1. Dialogues: The dialogues in each lesson are set at various authentic sites in China. The scenarios are intended to be typical of those encountered by foreigners conducting business in P. R. China. Authentic language of modern Chinese, which occurs in realistic business contexts, is employed to the greatest extent in order to provide the most efficient examples for students to imitate and eventually enhance their Chinese language proficiency.

2. Reading Passages: The reading passage in each lesson is a short essay, in which the topic of the lesson is further explored. The reading passages are intended to sketch some general pictures of cultural background in Chinese society and its business world. In the terms of language style, the reading passages in the book are in written form while the dialogues present a more lifelike spoken style.

3. Vocabulary and Patterns: The book presumes prior competence or mastery of about a 1000-word vocabulary. The Glossary of Beginning Level in Guidelines of Chinese Proficiency and the Degree of Difficulty of Chinese Characters, which has a 1033-word vocabulary of the most frequently used words, has been adopted as the measure to establish the vocabulary glosses for each lesson. The words that are not covered in this 1033-word vocabulary glossary are considered as new words for the book. Due to the fact that there is no supporting data of lexicostatistics in business Chinese, it was very difficult to decide what vocabulary items should be included. In order to better equip students with useful business terms in Chinese, a great effort has been made to select proper vocabulary words from a practical standpoint of conducting business. We therefore would welcome the input of teachers and students alike, so that we can continue to best meet the needs of the changing context of Business Chinese in the classroom. The patterns are another component of this section. Normally eight to ten patterns are presented in each lesson. There are certain important patterns that students may have been exposed to in their prior study but that they might not have mastered. Each pattern heading is followed by two examples. The first one is drawn from either the Dialogues or the Reading passage while the second one serves as an additional example.

4. Exercises and Activities: Exercises and activities are designed to reinforce newly introduced vocabulary and patterns as well as to help students in understanding the content of the dialogues and the reading passage in each lesson. Some questions posed in this section require students to do research in business related topics by using various media sources, including the internet, while some questions are intended to lead students into discussions of cultural differences. Instructors

may choose to use these exercises in whole or in part, as written homework or as in-class oral exercises.

5. Appendix: Appendixes in each lesson provide examples of business documents in Chinese as well as other useful information such as a Customs Declaration Form, a Product Catalogue, an Order Sheet, a Letter of Credit, a Letter of Intent, a Contract, and Common Chinese Signs etc. Some of them are duplicates of the originals.

The book has also complied a General Appendix, which contains a complete English translation of all dialogues and reading passages, vocabulary, patterns, useful web sites, a map of China, and a bibliography. There are 1010 new words and 152 sentence patterns introduced in the book. All the texts, vocabulary and patterns are printed in both traditional and simplified characters. Through study of this textbook, students may attain an intermediate level of Chinese or higher.

This book was designed by Daoxiong Guan and Hsiao-jung Yu. Daoxiong Guan wrote the dialogues and the reading passages. He also made vocabulary and pattern glossaries and took the responsibility for finalizing the whole book. Hsiao-jung Yu created the exercises and activities. Shannon Lee Du translated all of the dialogues and the reading passages into English. We want to thank Professor Xiong Yan and Chen Xiuping (Jiangxi Finance and Economy University), who not only provided some valuable materials and examples of business documents but also proofread the first draft of the book. Our gratitude also goes to Mrs. Susan Chan Egan (Chartered Financial Analyst, former Vice President at Scudder, Stevens & Clark, Inc.). Her special knowledge in business solved many problems that we encountered during translating business terms into English. We owe a special thanks to Ms. Guo Li and Mr. Xu Gang (Peking University Press), who proofread the whole book. It would have been impossible to publish this book without their continuous support. Finally, we want to express our gratitude to our students at University of California, Santa Barbara. It was their love of Chinese that encouraged us to complete this book.

Daoxiong Guan
Hsiao-jung Yu
Department of East Asian Languages and Cultural Studies
University of California, Santa Barbara
May, 2000

主要人物
Main Characters

 美 方

史强生
美国国际贸易公司亚洲地区总裁
Johnson Smith, CEO of Asia Region,
American International Trading Company

白琳
美国国际贸易公司亚洲地区总裁助理
Lynn Petty, Assistant to CEO of Asia Region,
American International Trading Company

 中 方

王国安
中国东方进出口公司总经理
Wang Guo'an, President,
China Eastern Import & Export Corporation

李信文
中国东方进出口公司副总经理
Li Xinwen, Vice President,
China Eastern Import & Export Corporation

张 红
中国东方进出口公司公共关系部主任
Zhang Hong, Director of Public Relations,
China Eastern Import & Export Corporation

目 录
Contents

1 到达中国 Arrival in China

（一）对话 Dialogue　/ 1
　　1. 入境 Entry　2. 见面 Meeting Each Other
（二）阅读短文 Reading Passage　/ 6
　　在中国，说中文 When in China, Speak Chinese
（三）练习与活动 Exercises & Activities　/ 8
（四）附录 Appendix　/ 21
　　1. 入境登记卡 Arrival Form
　　2. 海关申报单 Customs Declaration Form
　　3. 机场常见标志 Common Signs at Airport

2 在酒店 At the Hotel

（一）对话 Dialogue　/ 24
　　1. 旅客登记 Checking In　2. 酒店的服务 Hotel Services
（二）阅读短文 Reading Passage　/ 29
　　中国的旅馆 Chinese Hotels
（三）练习与活动 Exercises & Activities　/ 32
（四）附录 Appendix　/ 45
　　1. 旅客登记表 Hotel Guest Registration Form
　　2. 境外人员临时住宿登记表
　　　Registration Form of Temporary Residency for Visitors
　　3. 旅馆押金收据 The Deposit Receipt

3 正式见面 Formal Meeting — 48

（一）对话 Dialogue　/ 48
　　1. 问候和介绍 Greetings and Introductions
　　2. 说明访问目的 Explaining the Objectives of the Visit

（二）阅读短文 Reading Passage　/ 53
　　宾主见面的礼仪 Etiquette of Meeting for Guests and Hosts

（三）练习与活动 Exercises & Activities　/ 56

（四）附录 Appendix　/ 67
　　1. 常见职称、头衔 Common Job Titles and Official Titles
　　2. 名片实例 Samples of Business Cards

4 日程安排 Itinerary Arrangements — 69

（一）对话 Dialogue　/ 69
　　1. 讨论日程安排 Discussing Itinerary Arrangements
　　2. 修改日程安排 Revising Itinerary Arrangements

（二）阅读短文 Reading Passage　/ 73
　　吃得好、玩儿得好、生意做得好 Eat Well, Have Fun and Do Well in Business

（三）练习与活动 Exercises & Activities　/ 76

（四）附录 Appendix　/ 87
　　1. 日程表 Itinerary
　　2. 中国旅游地图 China Travel Map

5 出席宴会 Attending a Banquet /89

（一）对话 Dialogue / 89
    1. 请坐，请坐，请上座 Please Take the Seats of Honor
    2. 干杯，干杯！ Cheers!

（二）阅读短文 Reading Passage / 94
    中国人的宴会 Chinese Banquets

（三）练习与活动 Exercises & Activities / 97

（四）附录 Appendix / 106
    菜单实例 Sample Menu

6 初步洽谈 Preliminary Negotiations /109

（一）对话 Dialogue / 109
    1. 介绍产品 Introducing Products
    2. 询问价格 Inquiring Prices

（二）阅读短文 Reading Passage / 113
    货比三家不吃亏 It Pays to Shop Around

（三）练习与活动 Exercises & Activities / 116

（四）附录 Appendix / 128
    1. 产品目录 Product Catalogue
    2. 时装设计 Fashion Design

7 参观工厂 Visiting a Factory — 129

（一）对话 Dialogue / 129
　　1. 在会客室 In the Reception Room
　　2. 在生产区 At the Production Area

（二）阅读短文 Reading Passage / 134
　　中国的企业 Chinese Enterprises

（三）练习与活动 Exercises & Activities / 138

（四）附录 Appendix / 148
　　2017年中国企业50强 Top 50 Enterprises in China (2017)

8 价格谈判 Price Negotiations — 151

（一）对话 Dialogue / 151
　　1. 谈判成功 Successful Negotiations
　　2. 谈判失败 Failed Negotiations

（二）阅读短文 Reading Passage / 156
　　讨价还价 Bargaining

（三）练习与活动 Exercises & Activities / 158

（四）附录 Appendix / 169
　　1. 报盘信实例 Sample of Offer Letter
　　2. 微信截图 A Screenshot from WeChat

总附录 General Appendix — 171
　　课文英译（第1–8课）English Translation of the Text (Lesson 1-8) — 172
　　总词汇表（上册）Vocabulary Index (Volume I) — 188
　　句型表（上册）The List of Sentence Patterns (Volume I) — 205

1 到达中国
Arrival in China

史强生先生和白琳小姐是美国国际贸易公司的代表。这次他们来中国做生意。史先生过去在台湾工作过两年。白小姐去年来过北京，跟东方进出口公司的李先生认识。史先生和白小姐说中文说得都很好。

（一）对话 Dialogue

1. 入境 Entry

（在海关）

海关官员：您好！您是来旅行的吗？

史强生：不，我是来做生意的。这是我的护照和入境登记卡。

海关官员：这两件行李都是您的吗？请打开这个箱子。

史强生：好的，没问题。

海关官员：这些是什么？

史强生：这些是产品广告和货样，这一件是礼物。这些东西要交税吗？

海关官员：没有商业价值的广告和货样可以免税。超过两千元的礼物需要交税，您的没问题！不过，您还是需要填一张申报单。

白　琳：哦，这是我们的海关申报单，我的护照和入境登记卡。

海关官员：那是什么？

白　琳：那是我的好朋友！

海关官员：好朋友？

白　琳：（笑）是呀，那是我的电脑。我们总是在一起，是最好的朋友！

海关官员：（笑）你的中文真不错！

白　琳：哪里哪里！

课文英译

2. 见面 Meeting Each Other

（在机场出口）

白　琳：看，那是李先生！（招手……）李先生，好久不见了，你好！

李信文：你好，你好！白小姐，我们又见面了！欢迎，欢迎！

白　琳：我来介绍一下儿。这位就是东方公司的副总经理李先生。这位是我的老板，Mr. Smith。

史强生：您好！我是Johnson Smith，我的中文名字叫史强生。

李信文：您好！我叫李信文，欢迎您来中国！

史强生：谢谢！白琳常常跟我提起您，这次总算见面了！

白　琳：太好了！坐了十几个小时的飞机，总算到北京了！李先生，谢谢你来机场接我们。

李信文：不客气，我们是老朋友了。你们的入境手续都办好了吗？

白　琳：都办好了，一切都很顺利！

李信文：好，那我们走吧，车就在外边。我先送你们去酒店，你们一定都累了吧？

到达中国
Arrival in China

词汇（一） Vocabulary (1)

1.	到达	dàodá	to arrive
2.	国际	guójì	international
3.	贸易	màoyì	trade
4.	公司	gōngsī	company
5.	代表	dàibiǎo	representative; to represent
6.	生意	shēngyi	business; trade
7.	进出口	jìnchūkǒu	import and export
	进口	jìnkǒu	import; to import; entrance
	出口	chūkǒu	export; to export; exit
8.	入境	rù jìng	to enter a country
9.	海关	hǎiguān	customs
10.	官员	guānyuán	officer; official
11.	护照	hùzhào	passport
12.	登记卡	dēngjìkǎ	registration card
	登记	dēng jì	registration; to register; to check in
	卡	kǎ	card
13.	行李	xíngli	luggage; baggage
14.	箱子	xiāngzi	suitcase; box
15.	产品	chǎnpǐn	product
16.	广告	guǎnggào	advertisement; commercial
17.	货样	huòyàng	merchandise/product sample
18.	交税	jiāo shuì	to pay taxes/customs duties
19.	商业价值	shāngyè jiàzhí	commercial value
	商业	shāngyè	commerce; trade; business
	价值	jiàzhí	value

20.	免税	miǎn shuì	to exempt from taxation; tax-free; duty-free
21.	超过	chāoguò	to exceed; to surpass
22.	填	tián	to fill out
23.	申报单	shēnbàodān	declaration form
	申报	shēnbào	declaration; to declare (dutiable goods)
	单	dān	list; form; voucher
24.	招手	zhāo shǒu	to wave (the hands); to beckon
25.	副总经理	fù zǒngjīnglǐ	vice president; vice general manager
	副	fù	vice; associate
	总经理	zǒngjīnglǐ	president; general manager
26.	老板	lǎobǎn	boss
27.	总算	zǒngsuàn	finally; at last
28.	手续	shǒuxù	procedure; formalities
	办手续	bàn shǒuxù	to go through formalities/procedures
29.	顺利	shùnlì	smooth(ly)
30.	酒店	jiǔdiàn	hotel; wine shop

专有名词 / 特殊名词 Proper Nouns / Special Nouns

1.	史强生	Shǐ Qiángshēng	a name
2.	白 琳	Bái Lín	a name
3.	美国国际贸易公司	Měiguó Guójì Màoyì Gōngsī	American International Trading Company
4.	台湾	Táiwān	Taiwan
5.	东方进出口公司	Dōngfāng Jìnchūkǒu Gōngsī	Eastern Import & Export Corporation
6.	李信文	Lǐ Xìnwén	a name

句型（一） Sentence Patterns (1)

1. 是来 / 去……的　(express purpose in coming or going)

例：① 您是来旅行的吗？
　　② 我是去中国做生意的。

2. ……真不错!　... is not bad; ... is very good

例：① 您的中文真不错！
　　② 机场的服务真不错！

3. 就
(an adverb, serves as an emphatic marker; it is usually stressed in speaking)

例：① 这位就是东方公司的副总经理李先生。
　　② 我的车就在外边。

4. 提起……　to mention... ; to speak of...

例：① 白琳常常跟我提起您。
　　② 提起这种产品，这次我带了一个货样。

5. 谢谢 + clause　thank + clause

例：① 谢谢你来机场接我们。
　　② 李先生，谢谢（您）帮我们订了酒店。

(二) 阅读短文　Reading Passage

在中国，说中文
When in China, Speak Chinese

课文英译

在中国，说中文，会有很多好处。一句最简单的"你好"，常常使事情变得容易。"你好"让严肃的官员对你微笑，让紧张的谈判变得轻松。不要担心你说中文说得不好。你会发现，当你说中文的时候，中国人总是非常高兴，也更乐意帮助你。

说中文容易交朋友。有了好朋友，做生意、办事情都会有很多方便。只要你每天都说中文，能说多少就说多少，你的中文就会越来越好。

词汇（二）　Vocabulary (2)

1.	使	shǐ	to make; to cause
2.	变得	biànde	have become; to turn (into)
3.	严肃	yánsù	serious; solemn; stern
4.	微笑	wēixiào	to smile; smile
5.	紧张	jǐnzhāng	nervous; tense
6.	谈判	tánpàn	negotiations; talks; to negotiate

7. 轻松	qīngsōng	relaxed; light
8. 担心	dān xīn	to worry; to feel anxious
9. 乐意	lèyì	to be willing/happy to
10. 交朋友	jiāo péngyou	to make friends
11. 办事情	bàn shìqing	to attend to matters; to handle affairs
12. 越来越	yuèláiyuè	more and more

句型（二） Sentence Patterns (2)

1. 使 / 让　to make; to cause

例：❶ 一句最简单的"你好"，常常使（/让）事情变得容易。
　　❷ 他说的话使（/让）那位官员很生气。

2. 当……的时候　when...

例：❶ 当你说中文的时候，中国人总是非常高兴。
　　❷ 当我走到出口的时候，我看见李先生正在等我。

3. 只要……，就……　as long as... then...

例：❶ 只要你每天都说中文，你的中文就会越来越好。
　　❷ 只要我有时间，我就一定去飞机场接你。

4. 能 + V. + 多少 + 就 + V. + 多少　to V. as much/many as one can

例：❶ 你应该每天练习说中文，能说多少就说多少。
　　❷ 这些产品，我们能卖多少就卖多少。

5. 越来越……　more and more

例：❶ 他的中文越来越好。
　　❷ 现在去中国做生意的人越来越多。

(三) 练习与活动　Exercises & Activities

I. 词汇练习　Vocabulary Exercises

1. 连词比赛。 Matching games.

按照拼音找出相应的英文并将标示该英文的字母填进"？"栏，再写出汉字。
Match each *pinyin* with its English equivalent by filling in the corresponding letter into the "?" box, and then write Chinese characters into the "汉字" box.

* 第一场 Game one:

	PINYIN	汉字	?
1	màoyì		
2	dàibiǎo		
3	gōngsī		
4	guǎnggào		
5	jiàzhí		
6	shāngyè		
7	huòyàng		
8	chǎnpǐn		
9	guójì		
10	hùzhào		

	English equivalent
A	product
B	value
C	trade
D	passport
E	merchandise samples
F	representative
G	international
H	company
I	commerce
J	advertisement

* 第二场 Game two:

	PINYIN	汉字	?
1	jǐnzhāng		
2	tánpàn		
3	lèyì		
4	qīngsōng		
5	jiāo péngyou		
6	wēixiào		
7	bàn shìqing		
8	yuèláiyuè		
9	dān xīn		
10	yánsù		

	English equivalent
A	to smile
B	serious
C	to negotiate
D	to make friends
E	nervous; tense
F	relaxed
G	to handle affairs
H	to be willing/happy to
I	more and more
J	to worry

2. 用下面的词汇填空。Fill in the blanks by using words below.

> 护照　行李　交税　免税　官员　手续　产品　货样
> 海关申报单　入境登记卡　到达　价值　超过

　　当你_____中国的时候，你总是得办一些入境_____。例如，你应该准备好你的_____和_____；在海关，你还应该填写_____。你应该注意哪些东西要交税，哪些可以_____。比如，没有商业_____的_____广告和_____可以免税。价值_____两千元的礼品需要_____。如果你的_____很多，海关的_____也可能会问你一些问题。

3. 字谜。Crossword puzzle.

　　请根据下面的提示，猜一猜是哪个生词，把它的拼音填进下面的空格里，在旁边写出汉字，最后找出谜底。

Read each clue first, and then fill in the boxes with *pinyin* of the word you guessed. You may write the characters next to each clue. Once you fill out all the boxes, find out what "the wonder word" is.

The wonder word

提示 (Clues):　　　　　　　　　　　　　汉字

（1）不用交税　　　→
（2）进入一个国家　　→
（3）国际旅行时需要的证件　→
（4）买产品或者卖产品　→
（5）告诉海关你带了什么东西　→
（6）旅行时住的地方　→
（7）旅行时带的箱子　→

4. 反义词。Antonyms.

（1）到达 ←→ 出发　　　　　（2）入境 ←→ _____
（3）打开 ←→ _____　　　（4）出口 ←→ _____
（5）交税 ←→ _____　　　（6）紧张 ←→ _____
（7）担心 ←→ _____　　　（8）方便 ←→ _____
（9）容易 ←→ _____　　　（10）顺利 ←→ _____

II. 句型练习（一） Sentence Pattern Exercises (1)

1. 用"是来/去……的"回答下面的问题。
Answer the following questions by using the pattern of "是来/去……的".

（1）甲：您是来中国做生意的吗？
　　　乙：不，_____。

（2）甲：她是去机场接公司客人的吗？
　　　乙：不，_____。

到达中国
Arrival in China

（3）甲：昨天李经理为什么又去北京了？

　　　乙：_____。

（4）甲（有一点儿紧张）：那位海关官员是来做什么的？

　　　乙：_____。

2. 你刚到中国，觉得很多地方和很多东西都很有意思。请用"……真不错"说说你喜欢的东西。

   You have just arrived in China and feel that there are many places and things that are interesting (and good). Make some sentences to express your impression by using the pattern of "……真不错".

   （1）_____。

   （2）_____。

   （3）_____。

   （4）_____。

3. 🎧 008 用"就"（as an emphatic mark）做练习。

   Doing exercises with the word "就" (as an emphatic mark).

   A 用"就"回答下面的问题：

   Answer the following questions by using the word "就".

   （1）甲：请问，哪位是美国来的史先生？

   　　　乙：_____。

   　　　　　(Hint: "I am right here!")

   （2）甲：你带的行李很多吗？

   　　　乙：_____。

   　　　　　(Hint: Just two pieces of luggage.)

   （3）甲：哪一个是您带的货样？

   　　　乙：_____。

   　　　　　(Hint: that one is.)

   （4）甲：从机场到酒店远吗？

   　　　乙：不远，_____。

   　　　　　(Hint: it is right next to the airport.)

11

B 2003年麦当劳开始了一次世界范围的品牌宣传促销活动。它使用的广告口号是"i'm lovin' it"！请你把它翻译成中文，再上网找出它正式的中文翻译，看看是不是一样。

"i'm lovin' it" is an international branding campaign launched by McDonald's Corporation in late 2003. Think about how to convert it into Chinese first, then find the Chinese version (translation) of this slogan by using the internet and compare your version with the official Chinese version.

你的翻译：_____

The official Chinese version: _____

4. 请把下面的句子用中文说出来。在你的句子里一定要用上"提起……"。
Can you say the following sentences in Chinese? Please make sure to use "提起……" in your sentences.

（1）Speaking of our trip to China, everything went smoothly.

_____。

（2）My boss often mentions that Chinese company. We hope that we can do business with them.

_____。

（3）I mentioned this problem to you last week.

_____。

（4）You didn't mention that your company wanted to see the merchandise samples.

_____。

到达中国 / Arrival in China

5. 请用"谢谢 + clause",对帮助你、关心你的人表示感谢。
Please use the pattern of "谢谢 + clause" to express your gratitude to those who helped you or were concerned about you.

(1) 你的朋友开车到机场接你。你对他说:

(2) 服务员把你的箱子送到你酒店的房间。你说:

(3) 昨天你借用了白小姐的电脑。现在你把电脑还给她。你说:

(4) 你病了。朋友来看你,送给你花儿。你说:

(5) 你刚到北京。东方公司的李先生去机场接你,还帮你订了旅馆,请你吃了晚饭。请用"谢谢 + clause"的句型写一张感谢卡送给李先生。
You just arrived at Beijing. Mr. Li, who is from the Eastern Company, picked you up at the airport, booked a hotel for you and treated you to dinner. Please write him a "Thank-You" card in Chinese with the pattern of "谢谢 + clause".

III. 句型练习（二） Sentence Pattern Exercises (2)

1. 从下面的方框（A/B/C）中选择合适的词组，再用"使"完成句子。
Make the "使" sentences by choosing the proper parts provided in the boxes below.

a 坐了十几个小时的飞机
　　严肃的海关官员
　　办手续很顺利
　　明天的谈判很不容易
　　白小姐带的东西价值超过了两千元

c 担心
　　很轻松
　　非常累
　　有一点儿紧张
　　又担心又紧张

b 代表们　李经理　大家　她　我

（1）_____
（2）_____
（3）_____
（4）_____
（5）_____

2. 用"只要……就……"完成下面的对话。
Complete the following dialogues by using the pattern of "只要……就……".

（1）甲：这个电脑可以免税吗？
　　　乙：_____。

（2）甲：明天你能去机场接东方公司的代表吗？
　　　乙：_____。

（3）甲：那家公司乐意买我们的产品吗？
　　　乙：_____。

（4）甲：怎样才容易跟中国人交朋友？
　　　乙：_____。

到达中国
Arrival in China

3. 用"能 + V. + 多少 + 就 + V. + 多少"完成下面的对话。
Complete the following dialogues by using the pattern of "能 + V. + 多少 + 就 + V. + 多少".

（1）甲：我很想说汉语，可是我担心说得不好！

　　乙：别担心，_____。

（2）甲：对不起，这次我们只能买这些。

　　乙：没关系，_____。

（3）甲：总经理，这次去中国，我们应该带几本产品广告？

　　乙：_____。

（4）甲：老板，明天的谈判可能谈不完这么多问题吧？

　　乙：_____。

4. 用"当……的时候"问一问这些人在飞机上做什么。
Use "当……的时候" to ask what the people are doing on the airplane.

例：问：当王先生喝可口可乐的时候，谢先生在做什么？

　　答：当王先生喝可口可乐的时候，_____。

第四排：大张 / 小明

第三排：史老板 / 史太太

第二排：白小姐 / 李经理

第一排：王先生 / 谢先生

（1）_____
_____

（2）_____

（3）_____

（4）_____

5. 用"越来越……"看图说话。
Describe the pictures below by using the pattern of "越来越……".

（1）　　两年前　　　　一年前　　　　今年

（2）　　　以前　　　　　　　现在

（3）

IV. 阅读、讨论和其他活动 | Reading, Discussion and Other Activities

1. 🎧 012 **根据课文对话回答问题。**
Answer the following questions according to the dialogues in this lesson.

（1）史强生和白琳以前去过中国吗？
_____

（2）他们这次到中国做什么？
_____

（3）入境的时候，他们要填哪些表？
_____

（4）他们带了公司的产品没有？
_____

（5）他们带的东西要交税吗？为什么？
_____

（6）为什么海关官员说白小姐的中文很好？
_____

（7）史强生和白琳谁是老板？
_____

（8）李信文先生是谁？为什么白琳认识他？
_____

（9）史先生知道李先生吗？为什么？
_____

（10）史先生、白小姐公司的名字是什么？
_____

（11）史先生和白小姐坐了多长时间的飞机？
_____

（12）史先生和白小姐入境的时候有什么麻烦吗？

_____

（13）李经理开车带史先生和白小姐去哪儿？

_____

2. 思考与讨论。 Points for Discussion.

这一课的阅读短文里说，"当你说中文的时候，中国人总是非常高兴，也更乐意帮助你"。你觉得这是为什么？请你谈谈你自己跟中国人说中文的经验并跟你的同学分享。

The Reading Passage in this lesson says, "You will find that when you speak Chinese, Chinese people will always be very pleased, and more than willing to help you." Why is this true? Could you please share your personal experiences of speaking Chinese with Chinese people?

_____
_____
_____
_____
_____
_____

3. 对照附录中的"机场常见标志"，找出下面标志的意义。

Referring to the Common Graphical Symbols Used at Airports in the Appendix, identify the following signs.

（1）_____ （2）_____ （3）_____ （4）_____

（5）_____　　（6）_____　　（7）_____　　（8）_____

4. 角色扮演。Role-playing.

根据下面给出的情境分别写两段小对话并表演。
Based on the situations given, create two dialogues and act them out.

（1）你们公司派你去机场接一位重要的客人。
Your company sent you to the airport to pick up an important visitor.

（2）在入境的时候，海关官员请你打开你的箱子。
You just arrived in China. At the customs, the officer asks you to open your suitcase.

5. 小任务。利用当地交通工具。Tasks: Using local transportation.

请从下面的任务中选择一个，然后上网搜索有关信息，完成任务。
Please choose one of the assignments below and search for information online to accomplish your task.

A 你将在这星期一早上到达上海浦东国际机场。你计划当天就到上海虹桥火车站坐高铁到苏州工业园区。你听说星期一早上常常堵车（dǔ chē / traffic jam）！你决定上网查一查从浦东机场到虹桥火车站应该怎么走最方便。请写出你的最佳选择。
You will arrive at Shanghai Pudong International Airport this Monday morning and plan to take the high speed train from Shanghai Hongqiao Train Station to Suzhou Industrial Park on the same day. You have heard that the traffic is terrible during this time. You have decided to use the internet to find out how to get to the train station from the airport by using local public transportation. Please write down your best choice.

B 下个星期你的同事要飞到中国北京出差。他预订了北京喜来登长城饭店。他想试试看如何利用当地的公共交通工具,自己从北京首都国际机场到这家饭店。请你为他提供两个选择。

Next week your colleague will be going on a business trip to Beijing, China. He will arrive at Beijing Capital International Airport. He has booked a room at the Great Wall Sheraton Hotel Beijing and he would like to get to the hotel by himself. Besides taking a taxi, there are several choices of using public transportation to get there. Can you provide two choices of using public transportation for him?

6. 快速复习。Quick review.

A 阅读下面的短文,复习学过的词汇和句型。
Read the following text and review vocabularies and sentence patterns that you have learned.

  坐了十几个小时的飞机以后,美国国际贸易公司的史先生和白小姐总算到达了北京。入境的时候,他们用中文填写了入境登记卡和海关申报单。中国海关有规定(guīdìng / regulation):不是自己用的东西,价值超过两千元人民币就要交税。不过,没有商业价值的广告和货样不必交税。史先生和白小姐这次是来中国做生意的,他们带了一些产品广告、货样和几件小礼品。这些东西都可以免税。

  在海关,一位严肃的海关官员请他们打开箱子,还用英文问了他们几个问题。史先生和白小姐用中文回答了他的问题,这使那位海关官员很高兴。他笑着说:"你们的汉语真不错!"史先生和白小姐发现,当他们说中文的时候,中国人总是非常高兴,也更乐意帮助他们。他们想,会说中文真有很多好处。史先生告诉白琳:"以后只要有机会,就要说中文。"

  顺利地办完了海关手续,史先生和白小姐走出机场。白小姐看见东方公司的李经理就在出口等他们呢。白小姐给史先生和李经理做了介绍。李经理说:"我看你们一定累了吧?"他请史先生和白小姐上车,送他们去酒店休息。

到达中国
Arrival in China

B 问答 Q & A：

（1）入境的时候，史先生和白小姐填写了什么？
_____

（2）他们带了哪些东西？这些东西需要交税吗？为什么？
_____

（3）那位海关官员为什么很高兴？
_____

（4）为什么史先生对白琳说"以后只要有机会，就要说中文"？
_____

（5）李经理在哪儿等史先生和白小姐？为什么李先生要先送他们去酒店？
_____

（四）附录　　Appendix

1. 入境登记卡 Arrival Form

外国人入境卡
ARRIVAL CARD

请交边防检查官员查验
For Immigration clearence

姓 Family name	名 Given names
国籍 Nationality	护照号码 Passport No.
在华住址 Intended Address in China	男 Male ☐　女 Female ☐
出生日期 Date of birth　年 Year 月 Month 日 Day	入境事由（只能填写一项）Purpose of visit(one only)
签证号码 Visa No.	会议/商务 Conference/Business ☐　访问 Visit ☐　观光/休闲 Sightseeing/in leisure ☐
签证签发地 Place of Visa Issuance	探亲访友 Visiting friends ☐　就业 Employment ☐　学习 Study ☐
航班号/船名/车次 Flight No./Ship's name/Train No.	返回常住地 Return home ☐　定居 Settle down ☐　其他 others ☐

以上申明真实准确。
I hereby declare that the statement given above is true and accurate.

签名 Signature _____

2. 海关申报单 Customs Declaration Form

中华人民共和国海关
进境旅客行李物品申报单

请先阅读背面的填表须知，然后在空格内填写文字信息或画√。

1. 姓名
   - 拼音
   - 中文正楷
2. 出生日期　　年　月　日
3. 性别　　男　　女
4. 进出境证件号码
5. 国籍（地区）
   - 中国　（香港　　澳门　　台湾　）
   - 外国
6. 进境事由
   - 公务　　商务　　旅游　　学习
   - 定居　　探亲访友　　返回居住地　　其他
7. 航班号/车次/船名　　8. 同行未满16周岁人数

我（我们）携带（有）：

9. （居民旅客）在境外获取的总值超过人民币5,000元的物品　是　否
10. （非居民旅客）拟留在中国境内的总值超过人民币2,000元的物品　是　否
11. 超过1,500毫升酒精饮料（酒精含量12度以上），或超过400支香烟，或超过100支雪茄，或超过500克烟丝　是　否
12. 超过20,000元人民币现钞，或超过折合5,000美元外币现钞　是　否
13. 动植物及其产品、微生物、生物制品、人体组织、血液及其制品　是　否
14. 无线电收发信机、通信保密机　是　否
15. 中华人民共和国禁止和其他限制进境的物品　是　否
16. 分离运输行李　是　否
17. 货物、货样、广告品　是　否

我已阅知本申报单背面所列事项，并保证所有申报属实。

携带有9-15项下物品的，请详细填写如下清单：

品名/币种	数量	金额	型号	海关批注

旅客签名　　　　　年　月　日

到达中国
Arrival in China

3. 机场常见标志 Common Signs at Airport

出发
Departures

到达
Arrivals

中转联程
Connecting Flights

登机口
Gate

安全检查
Security Check

行李手推车
Baggage Cart

出口
Exit

入口
Entry

行李查询
Baggage Inquiries

行李提取
Baggage Claim Area

售票
Ticketing

托运行李检查
Baggage Check

绿色通道
Green Channel
（无申报物品）
Nothing to Declare

红色通道
Red Channel
（有申报物品）
Goods to Declare

边防检查
Immigration

海关检查
Customs

卫生检疫
Quarantine

租车服务
Car rental

摘自《民用航空公共信息标志用图形符号》（MH 00051997）
Graphical symbols for use on public information signs of civil aviation

2 在酒店
At the Hotel

李信文为史强生和白琳在长城酒店预订了房间。这是一家五星级酒店，不但服务良好、设施完备，而且地点非常方便。白琳很喜欢这个地方，可是她也有很多问题。

 （一）对话 Dialogue

1. **旅客登记 Checking In**

服务员：您好！

李信文：您好！昨天我为这两位美国客人预订了房间。我姓李。麻烦您查一下儿。

服务员：您是东方公司的李先生吗？

李信文：对，我叫李信文。

服务员：请您的两位客人填一下儿旅客登记表。

李信文：我为你们预订的是一间标准间、一间套房。标准间一天六百五十块，套房九百块。

白　琳：哇，比去年贵了不少啊！请问，我可以用英文填表吗？

服务员：可以。不好意思，我需要看一下儿你们的护照。

李信文：客人需要先付房间押金吧？

服务员：是的。可以付现金，也可以刷卡。

史强生：我用信用卡吧。

服务员：好的。你们的房间在十九楼。这是房卡。电梯就在那边。谢谢！

白　琳：十九楼！太好了！那么高，风景一定不错！

2. 酒店的服务 Hotel Services

白　琳：你好，请问洗衣房在哪儿？

服务员：自助洗衣房在二楼。如果您需要洗衣服务，您可以把脏衣服放在洗衣袋里交给我，也可以把洗衣袋留在房间里，等一会儿我就来拿。

白　琳：谢谢！请问，你们有"叫醒"服务吗？

服务员：有。您只要打一二三七，告诉服务台您需要几点起床就行了。

白　琳：您知道哪儿可以用互联网吗？我得查一下儿我的邮件。

服务员：二楼的商务中心可以上网。如果您自己带了电脑的话，您的房间里就能免费上网，不需要密码。

白　琳：那可太好了！酒店里有健身房和游泳池吧？

服务员：当然有。坐电梯到顶楼，健身中心和游泳池就在那儿。

白　琳：（有一点儿不好意思）还有……您知道哪儿可以换人民币吗？

服务员：外币兑换就在大厅的服务台。

史强生：（笑）不好意思，请问餐厅在几楼？这位小姐问了这么多问题，肚子一定饿了！

词汇（一） Vocabulary (1)

1.	预订	yùdìng	to reserve; to book
2.	五星级	wǔxīngjí	five star ranking; five star
	级	jí	rank; level; grade
3.	良好	liánghǎo	good; well
4.	设施	shèshī	facilities; amenities
5.	完备	wánbèi	well provided; complete with everything
6.	地点	dìdiǎn	place; site; location
7.	旅客	lǚkè	hotel guest; traveler; passenger
8.	客人	kèrén	guest; visitor
9.	标准间	biāozhǔnjiān	standard room
	标准	biāozhǔn	standard; typical
10.	套房	tàofáng	suite
11.	哇	wa	wow; (expresses surprise)
12.	不好意思	bù hǎoyìsi	to feel embarrassed; sorry
13.	付	fù	to pay
14.	押金	yājīn	deposit; cash pledge
15.	现金	xiànjīn	cash
16.	刷卡	shuā kǎ	to swipe a card; to use a credit card
17.	信用卡	xìnyòngkǎ	credit card
18.	房卡	fángkǎ	key card; room card
19.	电梯	diàntī	elevator
20.	洗衣房	xǐyīfáng	laundry room
21.	自助	zìzhù	self-help; self-serving
22.	洗衣袋	xǐyīdài	laundry bag
	袋	dài	bag

在酒店
At the Hotel

23.	叫醒	jiàoxǐng	to wake sb. up (For instance: 叫醒服务 wake-up call)
24.	服务台	fúwùtái	service desk; front desk
25.	互联网	hùliánwǎng	internet
26.	邮件	yóujiàn	mail; email
27.	商务中心	shāngwù zhōngxīn	business center
	商务	shāngwù	business, business affairs
	中心	zhōngxīn	center
28.	上网	shàng wǎng	to access the internet
29.	免费	miǎn fèi	to be free of charge
30.	密码	mìmǎ	password; secret code
31.	健身房	jiànshēnfáng	gym
32.	顶楼	dǐnglóu	top floor; attic
33.	人民币	rénmínbì	RMB (Chinese currency)
34.	外币兑换	wàibì duìhuàn	foreign currency exchange
	外币	wàibì	foreign currency
	兑换	duìhuàn	to exchange; to convert
35.	大厅	dàtīng	lobby

句型（一）　Sentence Patterns (1)

1. 不但……而且……　not only... but also...

例：① 这家酒店不但服务良好、设施完备，而且地点非常方便。
　　② 白琳不但用了健身房，而且去洗衣房洗了衣服。

2. A 为 B + V.+ sth.　A V. + sth. for B

例：① 昨天我为这两位美国客人预订了房间。
　　② 请你为我们兑换一些人民币。

3. A 比 B + Adj. + rough estimation (or specific quantity)
A is + rough estimation (or specific quantity) + Adj. than B

例：① 哇，（今年）比去年贵了不少啊！
　　② 坐飞机比坐火车快了十个小时。

4. 如果……（的话），就……　If..., then...

例：① 如果您自己带了电脑的话，您的房间里就能免费上网。
　　② 如果不用信用卡，就得付现金。

5. 可 + Adj. + 了　(可 is an emphatic adverb)

例：① 那可太好了！
　　② 一天没吃饭，我的肚子可饿了！

（二）阅读短文　Reading Passage

中国的旅馆
Chinese Hotels

课文英译

　　在中国，旅馆又叫酒店、饭店或者宾馆。最好的旅馆是五星级旅馆，当然也是最贵的旅馆。像北京的王府井希尔顿酒店、上海的锦江饭店、广州的白云宾馆等等，都是这样的大旅馆。一般来说，三星和三星以上的旅馆设施比较完备，通常设有餐厅、礼品部、健身房、美容沙龙、洗衣房和商务中心等等。这些设施都很方便，尤其是商务中心。在那里你可以上网，发邮件，使用电脑、打印机和复印机。很多旅馆还提供外币兑换、订票、租车和当地游览等服务。如果你打算在中国住旅馆，最好请旅行社帮你预订或者直接上网预订。你也可以请朋友帮忙或者自己给旅馆打电话。

词汇（二）　Vocabulary (2)

1.	旅馆	lǚguǎn	hotel
2.	宾馆	bīnguǎn	hotel; guesthouse
3.	最好	zuìhǎo	best; had better; it would be best
4.	等等	děngděng	et cetera; and so on
5.	一般来说	yìbān láishuō	generally speaking
	一般	yìbān	general(ly); common(ly)
6.	通常	tōngcháng	normal(ly); usual(ly)

7.	设有	shèyǒu	to have; to include within
8.	礼品部	lǐpǐnbù	gift shop
9.	美容沙龙	měiróng shālóng	beauty salon
10.	尤其	yóuqí	especially
11.	使用	shǐyòng	to use
12.	打印机	dǎyìnjī	printer
13.	复印机	fùyìnjī	copy machine; duplicator
14.	提供	tígōng	to provide; to supply; to offer
15.	订票	dìng piào	to book tickets; ticket booking
16.	租车	zū chē	to rent a car; car rental
17.	当地	dāngdì	local
18.	游览	yóulǎn	tour; to tour; to go sight-seeing
19.	旅行社	lǚxíngshè	travel agency
20.	帮忙	bāng máng	to help; to give a hand

专有名词 / 特殊名词 Proper Nouns / Special Nouns

1.	王府井希尔顿酒店	Wángfǔjǐng Xī'ěrdùn Jiǔdiàn	Hilton Beijing Wangfujing Hotel
2.	锦江饭店	Jǐnjiāng Fàndiàn	Jin Jiang Hotel
3.	广州	Guǎngzhōu	*a city name*
4.	白云宾馆	Báiyún Bīnguǎn	Baiyun Hotel

句型（二） Sentence Patterns (2)

1. 像……等等　　such as...etc.

例：① 最好的旅馆是五星级旅馆，当然也是最贵的旅馆。像北京的王府井希尔顿酒店、上海的锦江饭店、广州的白云宾馆等等，都是这样的大旅馆。
② 这家旅馆提供很多服务，像外币兑换、订票、租车等等。

2. ……，尤其是 + N. (or nominal phrase)
..., especially + N. (or nominal phrase)

例：① 这些设施都很方便，尤其是商务中心。
② 他们入境的时候不太顺利，尤其是在海关申报的时候。

3. 最好 + V.　　had better do...; it would be best to do...

例：① 如果你打算住旅馆，最好请旅行社帮你预订或者直接上网预订。
② 您最好使用信用卡。

4. 请 A 帮 B + V. ……　　ask A to help B to do...

例：① 你也可以请朋友帮忙或者自己给旅馆打电话。
② 请您帮我预订两张去上海的飞机票（吧）。

（三）练习与活动　Exercises & Activities

I. 词汇练习　Vocabulary Exercises

1. 连词比赛。Matching games.

按照拼音找出相应的英文并将标示该英文的字母填进"？"栏，再写出汉字。
Match each *pinyin* with its English equivalent by filling in the corresponding letter into the "？" box, and then writing Chinese characters into the "汉字" box..

*第一场 Game one:

	PINYIN	汉字	?
1	miǎn fèi		
2	yùdìng		
3	mìmǎ		
4	shèshī		
5	lǚkè		
6	kèrén		
7	biāozhǔnjiān		
8	zìzhù		
9	tàofáng		
10	dìdiǎn		

	English equivalent
A	password
B	traveler; hotel guest
C	standard room
D	to be free of charge
E	self-help; self-serving
F	to reserve; to book
G	suite
H	place; site; location
I	guest; visitor
J	facilities; amenities

*第二场 Game two:

	PINYIN	汉字	?
1	tōngcháng		
2	fùyìnjī		
3	shǐyòng		
4	dāngdì		
5	tígōng		
6	yóuqí		
7	dìng piào		
8	lǐpǐnbù		
9	lǚxíngshè		
10	dǎyìnjī		

	English equivalent
A	copy machine
B	printer
C	normally
D	especially
E	to book tickets
F	travel agency
G	local
H	to use
I	gift shop
J	to provide

在酒店
At the Hotel
2

2. 填空组词。Fill in the blanks to build up words or phrases.

例：___上___ 网　　　___互联___ 网

（1）_____ 卡　　_____ 卡　　_____ 卡　　_____ 卡

（2）_____ 房　　_____ 房　　_____ 房

（3）_____ 金　　_____ 金　　_____ 金

（4）_____ 厅　　_____ 厅　　_____ 厅

（5）电 _____　　电 _____　　电 _____　　电 _____

（6）旅 _____　　旅 _____　　旅 _____

（7）自助 _____　　自助 _____　　自助 _____

（8）洗衣 _____　　洗衣 _____　　洗衣 _____

（9）服务 _____　　服务 _____　　_____ 服务

（10）_____ 中心　　_____ 中心　　_____ 中心

3. 字谜。Crossword puzzle.

请根据下面的提示，猜一猜是哪个生词，把它的拼音填进下面的空格里，在旁边写出汉字，最后找出谜底。

Read each clue first, and then fill in the boxes with the *pinyin* of the word you guessed. You may write the characters next to each clue. Once you fill out all the boxes, find out what "the wonder word" is.

1.
2.
3.
4.
5.
6.
7.
8.

The wonder word ↑↑

*提示 (Clues)：　　　　　　　　　　　　　　　汉字

（1）早上打电话给你，让你起床的服务　→

（2）把一国的钱换成另一国的钱　→

（3）不用现金，用它付钱、买东西　→

（4）中国钱　→

（5）不需要付钱　→

（6）特别的号码，不可以让别人知道　→

（7）运动、锻炼身体的地方　→

（8）住旅馆的时候，用它开门　→

4. 用本课学习的生词回答下面的问题。
Answer the following questions by using new words from this lesson.

（1）在中文里，"旅馆"还有什么别的名字？它们的意思都一样吗？
_____

（2）哪些词汇在住旅馆的时候可能有用？
_____
_____

5. 谐音字。 Homophonous words.

　　在这一课的对话里，旅馆服务员告诉白小姐叫醒服务的电话是1237。这是一个谐音（xiéyīn / homophonous）的号码。你能猜到它的谐音字吗？在中文里，你还知道哪些谐音的数字？它们代表什么？

　　In the dialogue of this lesson, a hotel attendant told Miss Lynn Petty that the phone number for "wake-up call" service is 1237. Actually, this number, especially the last digit "7", is intended to be homophonous with another word (or phrase) in Chinese. Can you guess what this number suggests? Do you know any other numbers that are homophonous in Chinese? What do they mean?

_____

在酒店
At the Hotel 2

_____
_____

II. 句型练习（一） Sentence Pattern Exercises (1)

1. 根据提示用"不但……而且……"造句。
   According to the given clue, make sentences with the pattern of "不但……而且……".

   （1）_____
   (After a long flight, they are very tired and hungry.)

   （2）_____
   (Once they arrive in Beijing, they plan to discuss business as well as take a tour.)

   （3）_____
   (This hotel has a convenient location and excellent services.)

   （4）_____
   (At the hotel's business center, hotel guests can use the internet for free and can also use a computer and printer there.)

2. 昨天老板告诉你，下个星期有两位从一家外国公司来的客人要来参观、访问你们公司。老板让你负责接待他们。今天老板叫你到他的办公室。他想知道你准备得怎么样了。请用"A 为 B + V. ……"说出你已经做了什么，还计划做什么。

   Yesterday, your boss told you that two important guests from a foreign company will visit your corporation next week. You have been assigned to arrange everything for this visit and make sure that your guests are happy. Today, your boss called you to his office. He wants to know what you have done so far and what else you plan to do for their visit. Use the pattern of "A 为 B + V. ……" to make your sentences.

   （1）_____
   （2）_____
   （3）_____
   （4）_____

35

3. 下面是新北京大饭店的房间价格表。请用"A 比 B + Adj. + specific quantity (or rough estimation)"比较平日和周末各种房间的价格。
The following is a list of room rates for the New Beijing Hotel. Use the pattern of "A 比 B + Adj. + specific quantity (or rough estimation)" to compare these room rates during weekdays and weekends.

新北京大饭店房价表

房型	主楼		西楼	
	周一至周四	周末	周一至周四	周末
标准间	380.00	420.00	300.00	320.00
套房	600.00	650.00	380.00	400.00
商务标准间	420.00	450.00		
商务套房	780.00	900.00		
总裁套房	1100.00	1650.00		

_____

_____

_____

4. 请用"如果……（的话）"完成下面的对话。
Please complete the following dialogues by using the pattern of "如果……（的话）".

（1）旅　　客：请问，我需要用现金先付旅馆押金吗？

服务员：_____。

(Hint: if you have a credit card...)

（2）旅　　客：请问，在哪儿可以用互联网？

服务员：_____。

(Hint: if you have a laptop...)

（3）旅　　客：旅馆里有健身房吗？

服务员：有。_____。

(Hint: if you need to use the gym...)

（4）旅　　客：啊……已经三点多了！餐厅还开吗？

服务员：对不起，餐厅两点半就关了。_____。

(Hint: if you are hungry...)

5. 完成下面带"可 + Adj. + 了"的句子。
Complete the following sentences with "可 + Adj. + 了".

（1）_____ 可忙了！

（2）_____ 可紧张了！

（3）_____ 可方便了！

（4）_____ 可容易了！

（5）_____ 可严肃了！

（6）_____ 可顺利了！

6. 复习"就"的用法。
Review the usage of the word of "就".

A 在第一课中你已经练习了如何使用"就"。请你找一找在本课的第二个对话里有多少个"就"字，再想一想在这些句子里为什么用了"就"。

You have practiced how to use the word "就" in Lesson 1. Now please find out how many times the word "就" is being used in the second dialogues of this lesson, and think about why it has been used in those sentences.

B 一家国际鞋业有限公司计划提高在中国的产品销售（xiāoshòu/sales）。你的任务是帮助把这家公司的产品广告"Going all over the world; This is all I need!"翻译成中文。你的翻译必须使用"就"字。

An international footwear holdings limited company plans to boost sales in China. You have been asked to translate their advertisement "Going all over the world; This is all I need!" into Chinese. Please using the word "就" properly in your translation.

你的翻译：_____

III. 句型练习（二） Sentence Pattern Exercises (2)

1. 用"像……等等"完成下面的练习。
   Use the pattern of "像……等等" to accomplish the following tasks.

   （1）当旅客到达中国的时候，需要办一些手续。请举例说明。
   _____

   （2）举例说明一家三星或者三星以上的旅馆，通常有哪些设施、为旅客提供哪些服务。
   _____

   （3）告诉你的朋友，在中国哪些地方有意思。请举例说明。
   _____

   （4）告诉你的朋友在中国说中文的话会有很多好处。请举例说明。
   _____

2. 想一想，怎样用中文和句型"……，尤其是 + N.（or nominal phrase）"把下面的句子说出来？
   How do you say the following sentences in Chinese with the pattern "……，尤其是 + N. (or nominal phrase)"?

   （1）Traveling by airplane always makes me tired, especially international travel.
   _____

   （2）I love Chinese food, especially Beijing roasted duck!
   _____

   （3）These products are very expensive, especially this year's new product.
   _____

   （4）Generally speaking, Chinese are friendly to foreigners, especially when you speak Chinese to them.
   _____

在酒店
At the Hotel

3. 根据下面的要求，用"最好 + V."造句。
Use the pattern of "最好 + V." to accomplish the following tasks.

（1）下个月，你的朋友要去中国商务旅行。他想知道他应该怎样准备这次旅行。

　　你告诉他：_____。

（2）你朋友打算在北京待一个星期。你觉得他应该住在哪儿？

　　你告诉他：_____。

（3）你朋友想知道他在中国的时候怎样跟你联系最方便。

　　你告诉他：_____。

（4）你朋友还想知道怎样才能跟中国人交朋友。

　　你告诉他：_____。

4. 根据下面的要求，用"请 A 帮 B + V. ……"造句。
Use the pattern of "请 A 帮 B + V. ……" to accomplish the following tasks.

（1）你给旅行社打电话，要预订两张到上海的飞机票。（不要忘了告诉旅行社你要哪天去。）

　　你说：_____。

（2）在机场，你看见设有"外币兑换"的窗口（chuāngkǒu / window）。你想换500美元的人民币。

　　你说：_____。

（3）你告诉旅馆服务员你忘了带你的房卡。（你觉得很不好意思。）

　　你说：_____。

（4）你的房间就在电梯旁边，你不太喜欢。所以你给酒店服务台打电话，告诉他们你希望换一间房间。

　　你说：_____。

IV. 阅读、讨论和其他活动　Reading, Discussion and Other Activities

1. 根据课文对话回答问题。
Answer the following questions according to the dialogues in this lesson.

（1）李先生为史强生和白琳预订了什么样的房间？

（2）他们的房间多少钱一天？

（3）住旅馆的时候，客人需要办什么手续？

（4）他们需要付押金吗？

（5）如果客人有脏衣服需要洗，他们可以怎么办？

（6）这家旅馆的"叫醒"服务电话是多少？

（7）旅馆的客人可以在哪儿用互联网？

（8）这家旅馆有外币兑换服务吗？在哪儿？

（9）这家旅馆有健身房吗？在哪儿？

（10）在课文中，有三次用了"不好意思"。它们的意思一样吗？

2. 根据本课的阅读短文选出正确的答案。
Choose the correct answers to the following questions according to the Reading Passage in this lesson.

（1）上海的锦江饭店是一家五星级旅馆。　　　　　　　　对　不对

（2）在中国，旅馆也叫酒店或者饭店。　　　　　　　　　对　不对

（3）在中国，五星级旅馆都叫饭店。　　　　　　　　　　对　不对

（4）在中国，很多三星和三星级以上旅馆的设施也很不错。对　不对

（5）在旅馆的商务中心，客人可以租车和订票。　　　　　对　不对

（6）如果要在中国住旅馆，最好的办法是自己直接给旅馆　对　不对
　　　打电话。

3. 角色扮演。 Role-playing.

　　你正在旅馆的服务台填旅客登记表、拿房卡。你也问了很多问题。请参考使用下面的酒店示意图写出你和服务台服务员的对话并表演。

　　You check in at the hotel front desk. You ask a lot of questions too. Please create a dialogue by referring to the sketch maps of the hotel below, and then act it out.

（顶楼示意图）

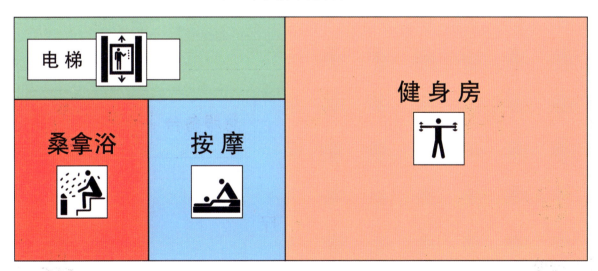

（十八楼示意图）

（二楼示意图）

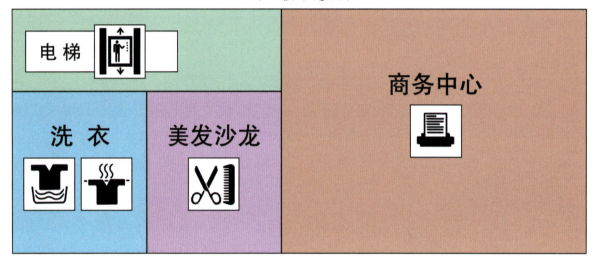

（一楼大厅示意图）

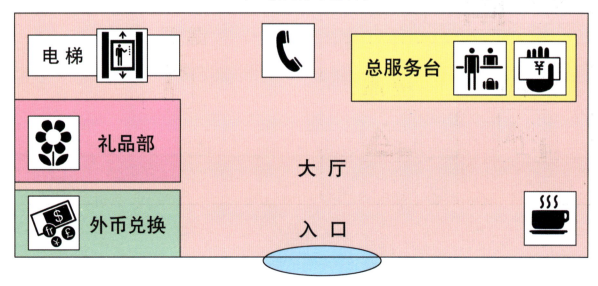

4. 小任务。Tasks.

A 上网找出一家三星或三星级以上的中国旅馆，了解这家旅馆的基本情况（例如地点、房间价格、服务和设施、旅客评价以及其他情况），把这些都写下来，在课上报告。你也可以跟你们国家的一家相同星级旅馆做比较。

Use an internet search engine to find a three-star hotel (or better) in China, get necessary information about this hotel's location, room price, service, amenities, travelers' review and etc., then report them in class. You may compare this hotel with a same category hotel in your country.

B 预订酒店 Make a hotel reservation

你和你的老板将要去北京（或上海）洽谈生意。你们要在那儿住一个星期。老板要你在网上找一家四星级酒店，预订两个房间。请跟你的同学2-3个人一组，共同完成这个任务。你们需要在课堂上报告你们打算预订的酒店，并说明理由。

Your boss and you will travel to Beijing (or Shanghai) on a business trip. You plan to stay there for a week. Your boss wants you to find a 4-star hotel online and reserve 2 rooms. Please work with one or two of your classmates and accomplish this task together. You need to make a report on the hotel you plan to reserve in the class and explain why your group has chosen this hotel.

请注意 Please note：

1. 酒店的地点 The location of the hotel:

请尽可能找一家位于北京中央商务区（或者上海浦东地区）的酒店，最好在国际贸易中心（或者上海国际金融中心）附近。你们要去的几家公司都在那一带。

Please do your best to find a hotel located in the Beijing Central Business District (or Shanghai's Pudong area). It would be even better if the hotel is near Beijing's China World Trade Center (or Shanghai International Finance Center/Shanghai IFC). The companies that you plan to visit are located in that area.

2. 酒店的设施和服务 The hotel's amenities and services:

（a）你的老板有每天锻炼的习惯，所以酒店应该有比较好的健身设施，例如健身房、游泳池等等。

Your boss is used to doing exercises every day. The hotel should have a gym and swimming pool, etc.

（b）你的老板还不太习惯吃中国菜，所以酒店内或者酒店附近最好有多家不同风味的饭馆可以选择。

Your boss is not used to Chinese food. It would be better if the hotel or nearby places have a variety of restaurants to choose from.

（c）酒店是否提供外币兑换、租车、洗衣等服务，房间内能不能（免费）上网等等。

The hotel should have currency exchange, car rental, laundry service and free internet, etc.

3. 酒店房间的价格 Guestroom price:

也许有一些五星级酒店正在以优惠房价促销。如果你能以四星级酒店的价格，订到一家符合以上要求的五星级酒店，老板一定会非常满意。

There might be some 5-star hotels having promotions. If you can book a 5-star hotel that matches all the conditions above at a price of 4-star hotel, your boss will be very happy.

5. 快速复习。Quick review.

A 阅读下面的短文，复习学过的词汇和句型。
Read the following text and review vocabularies and sentence patterns that you have learned.

长城酒店是一家五星级酒店。李先生已经为史先生和白小姐在这儿预订了一间标准间和一间套房。白琳去年来北京的时候，就住在这家旅馆。这次又回到这儿，她可高兴了。她告诉史强生她很喜欢长城酒店。她觉得这家酒店的地点很方便，去哪儿都很容易。她还告诉她的老板，这儿有商务中心、健身房、游泳池、美容沙龙、礼品部、餐厅等等，设施完备，服务也非常好，尤其是这家酒店的自助餐厅。如果可能的话，她打算每天都在这儿吃饭。史先生笑着说："如果每天都在这儿吃饭的话，我们最好每天都用健身房。"

在服务台，服务员小姐请他们先填一张旅客登记表。她还看了他们的护照。"欢迎你们来北京！这是你们的房卡，"服务员笑着说，"请问，您打算怎么付押金？"史先生回答说："刷卡吧。"史先生觉得用信用卡比用现金方便得多，他打算在中国的时候能用信用卡就用信用卡。可是白琳说她喜欢用现金。如果要付的钱很多，她才会用信用卡。她想在服务台兑换一些人民币。

B 问答 Q & A：

（1）住长城酒店，白小姐高兴吗？为什么？

（2）长城酒店有哪些设施？

（3）白琳最喜欢长城酒店的什么地方？

（4）为什么史先生说"我们最好每天都用健身房"？

（5）在服务台，他们办了哪些手续？

（6）为什么史先生打算用信用卡？

（7）白琳为什么要兑换人民币？她不用信用卡吗？

（四）附录　Appendix

1. **旅客登记表** Hotel Guest Registration Form

阳光假日宾馆

日期：　年　月　日			№0000001	
客人姓名		证件号码		第一联存根（白）
房　号		房　费		
到店日期		离店日期		
押金金额	¥：	金额大写	万　仟　佰　拾　元	
付款方式	□现金　□信用卡	联系电话		
会员卡号		客人签名		第二联客户（红）
备注：				

宾客须知：* 退房时间 12:00 前，超过 12 点加收半天房费，下午 6 点收全天房费。
　　　　　* 贵重物品请随身携带。* 结账时请交回房门卡，遗失照价赔偿。* 账务当天结清。

地址：××××××××××××　　　　当班收银员：
电话：××××××××××××

2. 境外人员临时住宿登记表
Registration Form of Temporary Residency for Visitors

临时住宿登记表
REGISTRATION FORM OF TEMPORARY RESIDENCE

英文姓 Surname	英文名 First ame	性别 Sex
中文姓名 Name in chinese	国籍 Nationality	出生日期 Date of birth
证件种类 Type of certificate	证件号码 Certificate No.	证件种类 Type of visa
签证有效期 Valid visa	抵店日期 Date of arrival	离店日期 Date of departure
何处来 Arr. from	何处去 Dept. to	停留事由 Object of stay
接待单位 Company	房号 Room No.	

请用正楷书写 Please write in block letters

离店时我的账目将以下列方式结算
On checking out my account will be settled by

☐ 现金 Cash   (   )   ☐ 信用卡 Credit Card
☐ 其他 Others   (   )   ☐ 旅行社凭证 T/A Voucher

为 Pay for Room No. _____ 房间承担账务

由 Pay by _____ 房间承担账务

注意 \ Remarks \ Name in Chinese 一 > 您可以将贵重物品存放在保险箱内。 二 > 退房时间为中午 12:00 整。 a> Please keep the valuable in safety box. b> Checking out time is 12:00 noon. 1> 2>	房价 Room Rate
宾客签名 Guest signature	职员签名 Clerk initial

GS 0014

在酒店
At the Hotel

3. 旅馆押金收据 The Deposit Receipt

庭苑商务宾馆
TINGYUAN SHANGWU BINGUAN

押 金 收 据
THE DEPOSIT RECEIPT

№ 0000001

Date:
日期：　　年　　月　　日

订房电话：0510-86019099

Guest Name:
宾馆姓名 _____

Room No:
房号 _____

Room rate:
房价 _____

Amount
押金金额（大写）　　万　　仟　　佰　　拾　　元整　　￥：_____

Received By:
收款人 _____

一联存根（白）　二联客户（红）

When check out, please return this deposit receipt to the reception desk.
退房时，请将此押金收条交给总台。
The guest within three months after departure, if did not deal with the balance refund, will be deemed to be abandoned automatically.
客人离店后三个月内，如一直没有办理余额退款，将被视为自动放弃。

3 正式见面
Formal Meeting

今天是中美双方代表的第一次正式见面。王国安总经理代表东方进出口公司欢迎美国客人。史强生先生代表美国国际贸易公司向中方说明了这次访问的目的。

(一) 对 话 Dialogue

1. 问候和介绍 Greetings and Introductions

王国安：欢迎，欢迎！欢迎光临。

李信文：让我来介绍一下儿。这位是美国国际贸易公司亚洲地区总裁史强生先生；这位是他的助理，白琳小姐。这位是我们公司的总经理，王国安先生；这位是公共关系部主任张红女士。

史强生：幸会，幸会！你们好！（握手）这是我的名片，请多指教。

王国安：不敢当。这是我的名片，以后也请您多多指教！

史强生：哪里，哪里！

王国安：我们坐下谈吧。（倒茶）请喝茶。昨天晚上休息得好吗？

史强生：休息得很好。旅馆很舒服，服务也很周到。谢谢贵公司的安排。

王国安：别客气。这是我们应该做的。在北京期间，如果你们有什么问题的话，请随时跟我或者李先生联系，或者告诉张红主任。

张　红：这是我的名片。上边有我的办公室电话号码和手机的号码。

史强生、白　琳：谢谢，谢谢！

李信文：王总，白琳小姐是我们的老朋友了。去年夏天她来北京，也住在长城酒店。

王国安：太好了！白小姐，欢迎您再次来到中国！

白　琳：谢谢！上次李先生给了我很多帮助，我们合作得很愉快。我非常喜欢北京。

2. 说明访问目的 Explaining the Objectives of the Visit

史强生：这次我们来中国的目的是想跟贵公司洽谈一下儿今年秋季的新订单和签订代理合同的事情。另外，如果可能的话，我们也想参观几家工厂，看看生产情况。

王国强：好啊。我们想把第一次会谈安排在明天上午。参观工厂的事儿，李先生正在跟那边的主管联系。稍后让他把具体安排告诉你们。

白　琳：如果有时间的话，我们还希望能够去上海和深圳考察一下儿那儿的投资环境。

李信文：我想这些都没有问题。今天下午我们就可以讨论一下儿日程安排。

史强生：好的。我们很想把日程安排早一点儿确定下来。

张　红：今天晚上，王总打算请大家吃饭，欢迎史先生和白小姐。白小姐，晚上六点半我去酒店接你们，行吗？

白　琳：行！六点半我们在大厅等您。

词汇（一）　Vocabulary (1)

1.	正式	zhèngshì	formal(ly); official(ly)
2.	双方	shuāngfāng	both sides/parties (in negotiations, etc.)
3.	目的	mùdì	purpose; objective; goal
4.	问候	wènhòu	greeting
5.	光临	guānglín	presence (of a guest, etc.); to be present
6.	地区	dìqū	region; area; district
7.	总裁	zǒngcái	chief executive officer; CEO
8.	助理	zhùlǐ	assistant
9.	主任	zhǔrèn	director;
10.	女士	nǚshì	woman; lady; Ms.; Miss
11.	幸会	xìnghuì	to be honored to meet (sb.)
12.	名片	míngpiàn	business card; name card
13.	指教	zhǐjiào	to give advice/comments
14.	不敢当	bùgǎndāng	I don't deserve your compliment; you flatter me.
15.	倒	dào	to pour (tea, etc.)
16.	周到	zhōudào	attentive; considerate; thorough
17.	期间	qījiān	duration; period; time
18.	随时	suíshí	at any time
19.	合作	hézuò	to cooperate; to work together; cooperation
20.	洽谈	qiàtán	to talk over with; to negotiate; negotiation
21.	秋季	qiūjì	autumn
22.	订单	dìngdān	order sheet; order
23.	签订	qiāndìng	to conclude and sign (a contract, etc.)

24.	代理	dàilǐ	agency; representation; to act as agent; agent
25.	合同	hétóng	contract; agreement
26.	会谈	huìtán	talks; to talk
27.	主管	zhǔguǎn	person in charge; to be in charge of
28.	稍后	shāohòu	later
	稍	shāo	a little; a bit; slightly
29.	具体	jùtǐ	specific; particular; concrete
30.	考察	kǎochá	make on-the-spot investigation; observe and study
31.	投资环境	tóuzī huánjìng	investment environment
	投资	tóuzī	to invest; investment
	环境	huánjìng	environment
32.	日程	rìchéng	schedule; itinerary
33.	确定	quèdìng	to define; to determine; to settle; to decide firmly

专有名词 / 特殊名词 Proper Nouns / Special Nouns

1.	王国安	Wáng Guó'ān	a name
2.	亚洲	Yàzhōu	Asia
3.	公共关系部	Gōnggòng Guānxì Bù	Department of Public Relations
4.	张红	Zhāng Hóng	a name
5.	深圳	Shēnzhèn	a city name
6.	王总	Wáng zǒng	a short form for President Wang

句型（一） Sentence Patterns (1)

1. A 代表 B + V. ……   A + V. ... on behalf of B

例：① 王国安总经理代表东方进出口公司欢迎美国客人。
② 史先生代表美方说明了这次访问的目的。

2. 让 sb.（来）V. ……
let sb. V. / allow sb. to V. (usually provide some sort of service)

例：① 让我来介绍一下儿。
② 等一会儿让他把具体安排告诉你们。

3. 在……期间   during (a certain period of time)

例：① 在北京期间，如果你们有什么问题的话，请随时跟我或者李先生联系。
② 在这次访问期间，美国代表参观了四家工厂。

4.（sb. V.……的）目的是……   the purpose (that sb. V. ...) is...

例：① 这次我们来中国的目的是想跟贵公司洽谈一下儿今年秋季的新订单。
② 他去深圳的目的是考察投资环境。

3 正式见面 Formal Meeting

（二）阅读短文 Reading Passage

宾主见面的礼仪
Etiquette of Meeting for Guests and Hosts

课文英译

中国人总是习惯用握手来表示欢迎、感谢或者友好。宾主见面的时候，主人应该首先跟客人握手，表示问候。中国人不习惯互相拥抱。即使是老朋友，见面拥抱也会使中国人觉得不太舒服。

宾主见面的礼仪当然也包括说一些表示问候和客气的话。像"你好""您最近怎么样""很高兴见到你""幸会""久仰""请多指教"等等，都是常用的问候语和客套话。

很多中国人喜欢在初次见面的时候互相交换名片。别人给你名片的时候，你应该用两只手接，表示礼貌。名片既可以帮助你记住对方的姓名，又便于今后互相联系。顺便说一句，有些人喜欢在自己的名片上列出很多头衔。别担心，你只要记住他的第一个头衔就够了。一般来说，列在第一的头衔常常是最重要的。

词汇（二） Vocabulary (2)

1.	宾主	bīnzhǔ	guest and host
2.	礼仪	lǐyí	etiquette; rite; protocol
3.	首先	shǒuxiān	in the first place; first of all
4.	拥抱	yōngbào	to hug; to embrace
5.	即使	jíshǐ	even; even if
6.	包括	bāokuò	to include
7.	久仰	jiǔyǎng	a short form of "久仰大名" which means "I have heard your illustrious name for a long time."
8.	客套	kètào	polite formula; civilities
9.	初次	chūcì	the first time
10.	交换	jiāohuàn	to exchange; to swap
11.	礼貌	lǐmào	courtesy; politeness
12.	对方	duìfāng	the opposite side; the other party
13.	姓名	xìngmíng	full name
14.	便于	biànyú	easy to; convenient for
15.	今后	jīnhòu	from now on; henceforth; in the future
16.	顺便说一句	shùnbiàn shuō yí jù	by the way; incidentally
	顺便	shùnbiàn	conveniently
17.	列	liè	to list
18.	头衔	tóuxián	official title

句型（二） Sentence Patterns (2)

1. 习惯 + V.   be used to/accustomed to V.

例：① 中国人总是习惯用握手来表示欢迎、感谢或者友好。
　　② 我习惯每天七点起床。

2. 即使……也……   even (if) ... (still/also) ...

例：① 即使是老朋友，见面拥抱也会使中国人觉得不太舒服。
　　② 即使你没有东西需要申报，也得填海关申报表。

3. 既……又……   both A and B; A as well as B

例：① 名片既可以帮助你记住对方的姓名，又便于今后互相联系。
　　② 服务台既收现金，又可以用信用卡。

4. ……，便于……   (do sth. which would make) easy to; convenient for...

例：① 我们互相交换一下名片，便于今后联系。
　　② 请早一点儿告诉李先生您的打算，便于他做出日程安排。

（三）练习与活动　Exercises & Activities

I. 词汇练习　Vocabulary Exercises

1. 根据英文的意思，填上正确的汉字。
Fill the blanks with correct Chinese characters according to English equivalent(s) provided.

汉字	*提示 (Clues)：
A （1）主（　）	person in charge; to be in charge of
（2）问（　）	greeting
（3）订（　）	order sheet; order
（4）光（　）	presence (of a guest, etc.); to be present
（5）地（　）	region; area; district
（6）（　）裁	chief executive officer; CEO
（7）（　）定	to define; to determine; to settle; to decide firmly
（8）（　）作	to cooperate; to work together; cooperation
（9）（　）教	to give advice/comments
（10）（　）谈	to talk over with; to negotiate; negotiation
B （1）宾（　）	guest and host
（2）对（　）	the opposite side; the other party
（3）初（　）	the first time
（4）包（　）	to include

56

正式见面
Formal Meeting 3

（5）（　）换 ← to exchange; to swap

（6）（　）衔 ← official title

（7）（　）貌 ← courtesy; politeness

（8）（　）于 ← easy to; convenient for

2. 请根据拼音填写正确的汉字。
Fill in the blanks with the proper Chinese words based on the given *pinyin*.

（1）我休息得很好，＿＿＿＿ 很舒服。您的 ＿＿＿＿ 非常 ＿＿＿＿。
　　　　　　　　　　lǚguǎn　　　　　　　ānpái　　　　　zhōudào

（2）旅行 ＿＿＿＿ 还没有 ＿＿＿＿ 下来。＿＿＿＿ 我给 ＿＿＿＿ 再打个电话吧。
　　　rìchéng　　　quèdìng　　　　shāohòu　　lǚxíngshè

（3）我们计划去上海 ＿＿＿＿ 一下儿 ＿＿＿＿ ＿＿＿＿。
　　　　　　　　　kǎochá　　　　tóuzī　huánjìng

（4）请问，这件事是谁 ＿＿＿＿？我应该跟谁 ＿＿＿＿？
　　　　　　　　　　zhǔguǎn　　　　　　liánxì

（5）这是我的 ＿＿＿＿。请您多多 ＿＿＿＿。
　　　　　　míngpiàn　　　　　zhǐjiào

（6）＿＿＿＿新的 ＿＿＿＿ 和 ＿＿＿＿ 代理 ＿＿＿＿ 是我们这次访问的 ＿＿＿＿。
　　qiàtán　　dìngdān　　qiāndìng　　hétóng　　　　　　mùdì

（7）在中国，＿＿＿＿ 见面的 ＿＿＿＿ 是互相握手，不是互相 ＿＿＿＿。
　　　　　bīnzhǔ　　　　lǐyí　　　　　　　　　　yōngbào

3. 组词。 Build up more words or phrases.

Ⓐ 例：（具）体　（身）体

（1）（　）理　（　）理　（　）理
（2）（　）单　（　）单　（　）单
（3）主（　）　主（　）　主（　）

57

（4）（　）方　　（　）方　　（　）方　　（　）方
（5）（　）订　　（　）订　　（　）定　　（　）定
（6）客（　）　　客（　）　　合（　）　　合（　）

B 例：预订……→　　<u>预订酒店</u>　　<u>预订机票</u>

（1）正式……→　　_____　　_____

（2）签订……→　　_____　　_____

（3）交换……→　　_____　　_____

（4）洽谈……→　　_____　　_____

（5）确定……→　　_____　　_____

（6）……周到→　　_____　　_____

（7）……期间→　　_____　　_____

（8）……环境→　　_____　　_____

4. 用中文回答下面的问题。
Answer the following questions in Chinese.

（1）在这一课里，你学到了哪些职称（zhíchēng / job title）和头衔？你还知道哪些中文的职称和头衔？

_____

_____

（2）初次见面的时候，中国人习惯用一些表示客气的词，说一些表示问候的话。在这一课里，你学到了哪些？你还知道哪些？

_____

_____

_____

II. 句型练习（一） Sentence Pattern Exercises (1)

1. 用"A 代表 B + V. ……"完成下面的句子。你可以从本课的附录《常见职称、头衔》中选择合适的头衔，用在你的句子中。

Use the pattern of "A 代表 B + V. ……" to complete the following sentences. You may chose proper titles from the list of "Common Job Titles and Official Titles" (see the Appendix in Lesson 3) and apply them in your sentences.

（1）_____ 代表 _____ 欢迎 _____。

（2）_____ 代表 _____ 感谢 _____。

（3）_____ 代表 _____ 参加 _____。

（4）_____ 代表 _____ 说明 _____。

（5）_____ 代表 _____ 签订 _____。

2. 🎧007 根据下面的要求，用"让 sb.（来）V. ……"造句。

Use the pattern of "让 sb.（来）V. ……" to accomplish the following tasks.

（1）初次见面的时候，大家都不认识。你说：

_____

（2）在飞机场，你看见一位漂亮的小姐有很多行李。你想帮忙。你说：

_____

（3）你的朋友想要换一间旅馆房间，可是他的中文不太好。你愿意帮助他。你说：

_____

（4）你希望先把这次访问的日程安排好。你说：

_____

3. 完成下面带"在……期间"的句子。比如，说一说发生了什么或者做了什么。

Complete the following sentences that contain the pattern of "在……期间". For instance, you may tell what has happened or what has been done during the given period of time.

（1）在这次谈判期间，_____。

（2）在中国旅行期间，_____。

（3）在美国代表访问期间，_____。

（4）在上海和深圳考察期间，_____。

4. 🎧008 用"（sb. V.……的）目的是……"回答下面的问题。
   Answer the following questions by using "(sb. V. ……的) 目的是……".

（1）请问，您这次为什么来中国？
   _____

（2）下个月王总为什么要去美国？
   _____

（3）史先生为什么给李经理打电话？
   _____

（4）美国代表去上海和深圳做什么？
   _____

III. 句型练习（二） Sentence Pattern Exercises (2)

1. 🎧009 用"习惯 + V."回答下面的问题。
   Answer the following questions by using the pattern of "习惯 + V.".

（1）宾主初次见面的时候，中国人怎样表示对客人的欢迎？美国人呢？
   _____

（2）中国人常常喝茶还是喝咖啡？
   _____

（3）为什么史先生在旅行的时候一般不带很多现金？
   _____

（4）以前人们洽谈生意的时候一般怎样互相联系？现在呢？
   _____

（5）每个国家都会有一些自己的风俗习惯。如果你去中国旅行，你觉得你可能会对什么不习惯（/不习惯什么）？

2. 用"即使……也……"回答下面的问题。
Use the pattern of "即使……也……" to answer the following questions.

（1）去中国旅行很有意思，可是得坐十几个小时的飞机。你想去吗？

（2）我没有东西需要申报。请问，我也要填海关申报单吗？

（3）这家旅馆非常贵，可是它是最好的五星级旅馆。你愿意住吗？

（4）明天的日程安排是去参观工厂。如果你累了的话，就在旅馆休息休息吧。

3. 用"既……又……"回答下面的问题。
Answer the following questions by using the pattern of "既……又……".

（1）为什么很多人都喜欢用互联网（/因特网）订票和订旅馆？

（2）你上次住的那家旅馆怎么样？

（3）外国人在中国旅行可以使用信用卡吗？

（4）昨天的洽谈，中美双方谈到了哪些问题？

4. 用"……，便于……"回答下面的问题。
Use the pattern of "……，便于……" to answer the following questions.

（1）为什么很多人初次见面的时候，常常喜欢互相交换名片？

（2）为什么现在用手机上网的人越来越多？

（3）为什么应该早一点儿通知中方你的旅行计划？

（4）为什么去中国做生意应该学会说中文？

IV. 阅读、讨论和其他活动　　Reading, Discussion and Other Activities

1. 根据课文对话回答问题。
Answer the following questions according to the dialogues in this lesson.

（1）中美双方参加今天见面的有哪些人？

（2）双方代表见面的时候，他们互相交换了什么？

（3）史强生的头衔是什么？白琳呢？

（4）谁是张红？她的头衔是什么？

（5）为什么李先生告诉王总说"白琳小姐是我们的老朋友了"？

（6）美国代表这次来中国的目的是什么？

正式见面 Formal Meeting 3

（7）美国客人昨天休息得怎么样？
_____

（8）美方代表还想去哪些地方参观和考察？
_____

（9）今天晚上有什么安排？明天上午有什么安排？
_____

（10）美国代表在北京期间，如果需要帮助，可以跟谁联系？怎么联系？
_____

2. 思考与讨论。Points for Discussion.

A 你觉得为什么在宾主见面的时候中国人不习惯拥抱？
Why are Chinese not accustomed to hugging when a guest and a host meet?
_____
_____

B 初次见面的时候，为什么很多中国人喜欢交换名片？为什么有些人喜欢在名片上列出很多头衔？
What is the reason that many Chinese like to exchange their business cards when they first meet someone? Why do some people like to list a lot of official titles on their business cards?
_____
_____

3. 根据下面的这张名片回答问题。
Answer the following questions regarding the business card below.

（1）许先生有三个头衔。哪个头衔最重要？
_____

（2）从这张名片你还可以知道什么？
_____

4. 小任务。Tasks.

A 白琳觉得很不好意思。她忘了带自己的名片。你能帮白琳用中文做一张名片吗？当然，不要忘了也为你自己做一张名片。
Miss Lynn Petty was embarrassed. She forgot to bring her business cards! Can you make a Chinese business card for her? And then make a business card for yourself.

B 你在一家翻译公司工作。今天你的任务是把下面的名片翻译成中文。
You work at a translation firm. Today your work is to translate the following business cards into Chinese.

正式见面
Formal Meeting   3

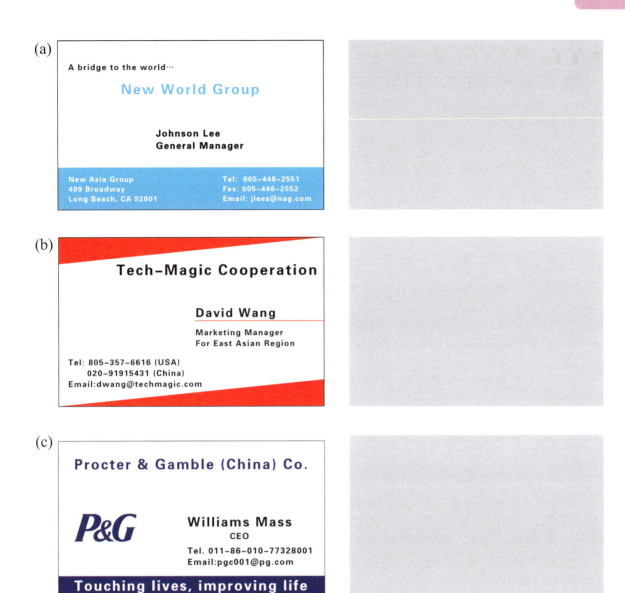

5. 角色扮演。Role-playing.

　　这个星期，一个外国贸易代表团来东方进出口公司访问。今天是双方代表的第一次正式见面。你为每个人做了介绍，双方交换了名片，互相说了一些表示客气的话。外国代表也向中方说明了他们来中国的目的。请用以上的内容写一个对话或者短剧在课堂上表演。

　　This week a trading delegation from a foreign country is visiting the Eastern Import & Export Company. Today both sides are having the first formal meeting. You introduced them to each other, and then everyone exchanged business cards. The visitors also gave a brief explanation about the main purpose of this trip. Write a short script about the occasion and act it out in class. Please include a dialogue and other background information related to proper manners, such as shaking hands, etc.

65

6. 快速复习。Quick review.

A 阅读下面的短文，复习学过的词汇和句型。
Read the following text and review vocabularies and sentence patterns that you have learned.

史先生和白小姐住进了长城酒店。他们发现这家旅馆既有周到的服务又有完备的设施，地点也很方便。他们用美元兑换了一些人民币，在商务中心使用了复印机，请洗衣房为他们洗了衣服。白琳在她的房间里上了网，还去健身房锻炼了一会儿。今天美方代表要跟中方正式见面。早上七点，史先生和白小姐就起床了。史先生没有用"叫醒"服务。他说他习惯早起床。不过，白小姐用了"叫醒"服务。她说她不习惯早起床。在北京期间，她可能每天都需要用"叫醒"服务。

李先生是八点来酒店接他们的。到了东方进出口公司，王国安总经理和张红主任已经在等他们了。李先生为双方作了介绍。王总说，他代表东方公司欢迎史先生和白小姐，希望他们的这次访问一切顺利。双方互相握手，交换了名片。大家都说了一些表示客气和问候的话，像"幸会""久仰""请多指教"等等。史强生注意到，即使是老朋友，中国人也总是握手表示问候，很少互相拥抱。他还注意到，王总经理的名片上列了五个头衔。他想王总一定是一位很重要的人。

今天的见面双方都很高兴。王总告诉史先生和白小姐，在他们访问中国期间，如果有什么问题的话，可以随时打电话给他或者李先生。

B 问答 Q & A：

（1）住进酒店以后，史先生和白小姐做了什么？

_____

（2）他们觉得这家酒店怎么样？

_____

（3）他们用了酒店的"叫醒"服务没有？为什么？

_____

（4）李先生是什么时候来酒店接美国客人的？

_____

（5）双方见面的时候，史先生注意到什么？

_____

（6）今天的见面顺利吗？见面的时候有问题吗？

_____

（四）附录　Appendix

1. 常见职称、头衔　Common Job Titles and Official Titles

工商企业 Industry and Commerce：

董事长	dǒngshìzhǎng	Chairman of the Board
常务董事	chángwù dǒngshì	Standing member of the board of trustees
董事	dǒngshì	Trustee; Director
总经理	zǒngjīnglǐ	President; General Manager
总裁	zǒngcái	President; CEO
经理/主管	jīnglǐ / zhǔguǎn	Manager; Department Chief
厂长	chǎngzhǎng	Factory Director; Factory Manager
总工程师	zǒnggōngchéngshī	Chief Engineer
工程师	gōngchéngshī	Engineer
审计师	shěnjìshī	Comptroller
会计师	kuàijìshī	Accountant

政府部门 Government Departments：

部长	bùzhǎng	Minister
司长	sīzhǎng	Department Director (at the state level)
厅长/局长	tīngzhǎng / júzhǎng	Department or Bureau Director (at the provincial level)
处长	chùzhǎng	Section Chief
办公室主任	bàngōngshì zhǔrèn	Office Director
科长	kēzhǎng	Office Chief

2. 名片实例 Samples of Business Cards

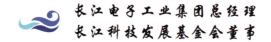

4 日程安排
Itinerary Arrangements

史强生和白琳计划在中国逗留一个星期左右。除了要在北京跟中方洽谈业务和参观工厂以外，他们还打算去上海看商品交易会、去深圳考察工业园区和一家创业公司。现在，李信文先生要跟他们一起讨论这几天的日程安排。

（一）对 话 Dialogue

1. 讨论日程安排 Discussing Itinerary Arrangements

李信文：史先生、白小姐，现在我们一起来谈谈日程安排，怎么样？

史强生：好啊。这次来中国，我们要办的事很多，想去的地方也不少，需要好好儿地计划一下儿。李先生，我们打算在中国一共待八天，您看时间够吗？

李信文：嗯，听起来时间确实有一点儿紧。不过，只要安排得合理，就应该没问题。

白　琳：李先生安排日程非常有经验。去年我在北京，他把每天都安排得满满的。上午洽谈业务，下午参观，晚上看表演，连给男朋友打电话的时间都没有！（笑）

李信文：（笑）对不起，白小姐。这次我们一定给你专门留出打电话的时间。

白　琳：没关系，不用了！反正现在我们已经吹了！

课文英译

2. **修改日程安排** Revising Itinerary Arrangements

李信文：这次的日程，我想这样安排：前五天在北京，后三天，两天在上海，一天在深圳。你们觉得怎么样？

史强生：在深圳只待一天，时间是不是太短了？听说深圳的投资环境很好，经济发展得很迅速，尤其是高新科技产业的发展。我很希望能有机会亲眼看看。

李信文：如果这样的话，我们可以把计划修改成在北京四天，上海和深圳各两天。行吗？

白　琳：我觉得这样比较合适。李先生，请问在北京的活动是怎么安排的？

李信文：在北京，除了洽谈业务以外，还要参观一家服装厂、一家玩具厂，游览故宫和长城。

史强生：这样安排很好、很周到。李先生，让您费心了！

李信文：没什么，这是我应该做的。另外，今天晚上七点是欢迎宴会；明天晚上，服装厂的钱厂长想邀请你们两位吃饭；后天晚上我想请你们品尝著名的北京烤鸭……

史强生：李先生，您太客气了！

白　琳：（对史强生说）现在你知道为什么去年我胖了十磅吧？（笑）

词汇（一） Vocabulary (1)

1.	逗留	dòuliú	to stay; to stop
2.	左右	zuǒyòu	about; around
3.	业务	yèwù	business; professional work;
4.	商品	shāngpǐn	merchandise; goods; commodity
5.	交易会	jiāoyìhuì	trade fair
	交易	jiāoyì	deal; trade; transaction; to deal; to trade
6.	工业园区	gōngyè yuánqū	industrial park
7.	创业公司	chuàngyè gōngsī	start-up company
	创业	chuàngyè	to start an undertaking; business start-up
8.	好好儿	hǎohāor	carefully; to the best of one's ability;
9.	待	dāi	to stay
10.	听起来	tīng qǐlái	to sound like; to sound as if
11.	合理	hélǐ	reasonable; rational
12.	专门	zhuānmén	specially; special; specialized
13.	反正	fǎnzhèng	anyway; anyhow; in any case
14.	吹	chuī	to blow; to play (a wind instrument); to break up (with boyfriend/girlfriend); to fall through (of plans)
15.	修改	xiūgǎi	to revise; to modify; revision
16.	发展	fāzhǎn	development; to develop
17.	迅速	xùnsù	rapid; speedy; prompt
18.	高新科技	gāo-xīn kējì	advanced and new technology
	科技	kējì	science and technology
19.	产业	chǎnyè	industry; estate; property
20.	亲眼	qīnyǎn	with one's own eyes; personally
21.	服装厂	fúzhuāngchǎng	clothing factory
	服装	fúzhuāng	dress; clothing
	（工）厂	(gōng) chǎng	factory

22.	玩具	wánjù	toy
23.	费心	fèi xīn	to give a lot of care; to take a lot of trouble
24.	没什么	méi shénme	it's nothing; it doesn't matter
25.	另外	lìngwài	in addition; besides
26.	厂长	chǎngzhǎng	factory director/manager
27.	邀请	yāoqǐng	to invite; invitation
28.	后天	hòutiān	day after tomorrow
29.	品尝	pǐncháng	to taste; to sample
30.	著名	zhùmíng	famous; celebrated
31.	磅	bàng	pound

专有名词 / 特殊名词 Proper Nouns / Special Nouns

1.	故宫	Gùgōng	the Imperial Palace
2.	长城	Chángchéng	the Great Wall
3.	北京烤鸭	Běijīng Kǎoyā	Beijing roast duck

句型（一） Sentence Patterns (1)

1. 除了……以外，还…… besides / in addition to..., also...

例：❶ 除了在北京洽谈业务以外，他们还打算去上海和深圳考察投资环境。
　　❷ 除了货样以外，他还带了几件礼物。

2. 连……都 / 也…… even / including...

例：❶（我）连给男朋友打电话的时间都没有！
　　❷ 我连电脑也带来了。

3. 反正　　anyway; anyhow; in any case

例：① 反正现在我们已经吹了！
　　② 没有带现金没关系，反正我有信用卡。

4. 把 sth. V. 成……　　V. sth. to/into/as...

例：① 我们可以把计划修改成在北京四天，上海和深圳各两天。
　　② 对不起，我把一百块看成十块了。

（二）阅读短文　Reading Passage

吃得好、玩儿得好、生意做得好
Eat Well, Have Fun and Do Well in Business

课文英译

中国地大人多，交通繁忙。外国人在中国旅行，不仅会有语言的问题，而且常常会遇到一些想不到的麻烦。如果你计划去中国出差，一定要安排好你的旅行计划。你可以把想要参观、访问、考察的地方通知你在中国的接待单位，请他们为你安排日程，预订旅馆、飞机票或者火车票。你也可以把你的日程表事先用邮件发给中方，便于他们做好接待准备。

无论你是去中国洽谈生意还是私人访问，游览和赴宴都是中国人日程安排中少不了的内容。尤其是频繁的请客吃饭，有时候甚至会成为一种负担。中国人觉得，请客吃饭有助于建立关系、发展友谊。请问，在吃了一顿丰盛的晚饭以后，有谁还能对主人说"不"呢？

词汇（二） Vocabulary (2)

1.	交通	jiāotōng	traffic; transportation; communications
2.	繁忙	fánmáng	(very) busy; hectic
3.	想不到	xiǎngbudào	unexpected
4.	出差	chū chāi	be away on official business or on a business trip
5.	接待单位	jiēdài dānwèi	host organization
	接待	jiēdài	to receive/admit a guest
	单位	dānwèi	unit; organization; place of work
6.	日程表	rìchéngbiǎo	schedule; agenda; itinerary
7.	事先	shìxiān	in advance; beforehand
8.	无论	wúlùn	no matter; regardless
9.	私人	sīrén	private; personal
10.	赴宴	fù yàn	to attend a banquet
11.	少不了	shǎobuliǎo	cannot do without; indispensable
12.	频繁	pínfán	frequently; incessant
13.	请客	qǐng kè	invite/entertain guests; treat sb. (to a meal)
14.	甚至	shènzhì	even (to the extent that ...); to go so far as
15.	成为	chéngwéi	to become; to turn into;
16.	负担	fùdān	burden
17.	有助于	yǒuzhùyú	be conductive/helpful to
18.	建立	jiànlì	to establish; to build
19.	顿	dùn	a measure word for meals
20.	丰盛	fēngshèng	rich; sumptuous
21.	主人	zhǔrén	host; master

日程安排
Itinerary Arrangements 4

句型（二） Sentence Patterns (2)

1. **不仅……而且……**   not only... but also...

   例：① 外国人在中国旅行，不仅会有语言的问题，而且常常会遇到一些想不到的麻烦。
   ② 我们今年的旅行不仅玩儿得很好而且吃得非常好。

2. **无论……还是……，（……）都……**   no matter... or...

   例：① 无论你是去中国洽谈生意还是私人访问，游览和赴宴都是中国人日程安排中少不了的内容。
   ② 无论您要订单间还是套房，我们都有。

3. **A 有助于 B**   A is conducive / helpful to B

   例：① 中国人觉得，请客吃饭有助于建立关系、发展友谊。
   ② 会说中文有助于跟中国人交朋友。

4. **……，有谁还能 / 还能不……呢？**   ..., what person still can / still can not...?

   例：① 在吃了一顿丰盛的晚饭以后，有谁还能对主人说"不"呢？
   ② 这么好的产品，有谁还能不喜欢呢？

（三）练习与活动　Exercises & Activities

I. 词汇练习　Vocabulary Exercises

1. 请根据拼音填写正确的汉字。
Fill in the blanks with the proper Chinese words based on the given *pinyin*.

（1）这次去中国洽谈 _____，我打算在上海 _____ 一个星期 _____。
　　　　　　　　　　　yèwù　　　　　　　　　　　dòuliú　　　　　　　zuǒyòu

（2）我计划考察那里的 _____，参观一个 _____。
　　　　　　　　　　　tóuzī huánjìng　　　　　　jiāoyìhuì

（3）谢谢您 _____ 帮我们 _____ 了旅行日程。现在的安排比较 _____。
　　　　　　fèi xīn　　　　　xiūgǎi　　　　　　　　　　　　　　　　　hélǐ

（4）我想 _____ 两家 _____ 公司，_____ 看看中国 _____
　　　　　　kǎochá　　　　　chuàngyè　　　　qīnyǎn　　　　　　　　gāo-xīn kējì

产业的 _____ 发展。
　　　　　xùnsù

（5）真不顺利！那份 _____ 已经 _____ 了！
　　　　　　　　　　　dìngdān　　　　　　chuī

（6）_____。_____ 我们还有另一家公司的合同。
　　　méi shénme　　fǎnzhèng

2. 字谜。Crossword puzzle.

请根据下面的提示，猜一猜是哪个生词，把它的拼音填进下面的空格里，在旁边写出汉字，最后找出谜底。

Read each clue first, and then fill in the boxes with *pinyin* of the word you made a guess. You may write the characters next to each clue. Once you fill out all the boxes, find out what "the wonder word" is.

日程安排
Itinerary Arrangements 4

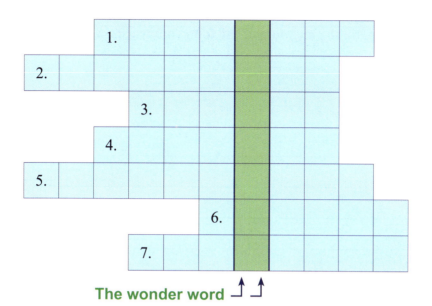

The wonder word ↑ ↑

* 提示 (Clues)： 　　　　　　　　　　　　汉字

（1）明天的明天　　　→

（2）试一试，看看好吃不好吃　　→

（3）很快，非常快　　→

（4）自己去看，不是听别人告诉你　→

（5）没关系，不重要　→

（6）小孩子玩的东西　→

（7）非常有名　　　　→

3. 用中文解释下面的词汇，再造句。
Use Chinese to explain the meaning of the following words, and then make a sentence.

例：频繁："很多很多次"的意思。

李经理频繁地给对方打电话，总算把事情安排好了。

（1）逗留：_____

_____

（2）吹：_____

_____

（3）费心：_____

_____

（4）亲眼：_____

_____

（5）高新科技：_____

_____

（6）请客：_____

_____

（7）事先：_____

_____

（8）出差：_____

_____

（9）少不了：_____

_____

（10）丰盛：_____

_____

日程安排
Itinerary Arrangements **4**

II. 句型练习（一）　　Sentence Pattern Exercises (1)

1. 用"除了……以外，还……"完成下面的句子。
Complete the following sentences by using the pattern of "除了……以外，还……".

（1）除了洽谈订单以外，我们 _____。

（2）除了参观交易会以外，美国代表 _____。

（3）除了为客人预订飞机票以外，李先生 _____。

（4）除了 _____ 以外，中美双方还签订了新合同。

（5）除了 _____ 以外，_____。

2. 🎧 007 用"连……都……"完成下面的对话。
Complete the following dialogues by using the pattern "连……都……".

（1）A：白小姐，我们去中国的日程都安排好了吗？

　　 B：别担心。我连 _____ 都预订好了！

（2）A：王总，昨天跟美国贸易代表的谈判顺利吗？

　　 B：非常顺利。我们连 _____ 都签订好了！

（3）A：哇，这么大的箱子，你一定带了不少东西！

　　 B：是啊，我连 _____ 都带来了。

（4）A：李经理，好几天没有看见您了。您最近忙吧？

　　 B：忙极了！这个星期我连 _____ 都没有时间！

3. 🎧 008 用"反正"回答下面的问题。请注意括号中给出的提示。
Answer the following questions by using the pattern "反正". Please pay your attention to the hints given in the brackets.

（1）A：不好，我忘了带信用卡！怎么办？

　　 B：_____

（Hint：Don't worry. I have a lot of cash!）

（2）A：对不起，今天大概没有时间去那家创业公司考察了！

　　　B：_____

（Hint：We have enough time to do it tomorrow anyway!）

（3）A：谈了一天生意，今天晚上我们休息休息，看个电影，怎么样？

　　　B：_____

（Hint：It sounds good! We don't have things to do tonight.）

（4）A：这家五星级酒店真漂亮！我们就住这儿吧！你说呢？

　　　B：_____

（Hint：Why not? The boss said that he is going to pay for it!）

4. 从下面列出的词语中选择四个，再用句型"把 sth. V. 成……"造句。
Choose four words from the below, and then use the pattern "把 sth. V. 成……" to make sentences.

"修改成 / 写成 / 说成 / 看成 / 听成 / 做成 / 画成 / 打（to type）成 / 翻译成"

（1）_____
（2）_____
（3）_____
（4）_____

III. 句型练习（二）　Sentence Pattern Exercises (2)

1. 🎧009 "不仅……而且……"和第二课里的"不但……而且……"都是很常用的句型。它们的意思和用法都一样。请根据下面的要求，用"不仅……而且……"造句。
   Both "不仅……而且……" and "不但……而且……" (*see it in Lesson 2) are very common sentence patterns in Chinese. Their meanings and usages are exactly the same. Use the pattern of "不仅……而且……" to accomplish the following tasks.

   （1）昨天的欢迎宴会非常丰盛。请用"不仅……而且……"说一说宴会上有什么菜。

   _____

   （2）在今天的洽谈中，双方代表谈到了很多问题。请用"不仅……而且……"说一说他们谈到了哪些问题。

   _____

   （3）请用"不仅……而且……"说一说为什么美国代表希望在中国多逗留几天。

   _____

   （4）外国人到中国做生意，常常会遇到一些想不到的问题。请用"不仅……而且……"说一说他们可能会遇到什么问题。

   _____

2. 🎧010 请参考提示，用"无论……还是……，（……）都……"回答下面的问题。
   Please refer to the hints provided in the brackets and answer the following questions by using the pattern "无论……还是……，（……）都……".

   （1）明天您打算参观服装厂还是考察玩具厂？

   _____

   （want to visit both places.）

   （2）中国人习惯跟新朋友拥抱还是跟老朋友拥抱？

   _____

   （No, Chinese are not used to greet people with hugs.）

（3）你觉得长城饭店的服务好还是假日酒店（Holiday Inn）的服务好？

_____

(the services at both hotels are good.)

（4）这件是礼物，那件是产品货样。请问我应该填海关申报表吗？

_____

(both items need to be listed on the form.)

3. 用"A 有助于 B"回答下面的问题。
Answer the following questions by using the pattern "A 有助于 B".

（1）会说中文有什么好处？

_____

（2）交换名片有什么好处？

_____

（3）为什么做生意的时候，请客吃饭常常是少不了的事？

_____

（4）为什么来谈生意的外国代表，常常希望参观、考察那些发展很快的中国公司和工厂？

_____

4. 用"……，有谁还能……呢？"或者"……，有谁还能不……呢？"回答下面的问题。
Answer the following questions by using the pattern "……，有谁还能……呢？" or "……，有谁还能不……呢？".

（1）为什么没有人买那种产品？

_____

（2）为什么大家都愿意跟那家公司做生意？

_____

（3）您看起来很累。怎么了？

（4）为什么住这家旅馆的客人总是这么少？

（5）为什么来中国的外国人都要去长城？

IV. 阅读、讨论和其他活动　Reading, Discussion and Other Activities

1. 根据课文回答问题。
Answer the following questions according to the dialogues in this lesson.

（1）史强生和白琳计划这次在中国逗留几天？

（2）李信文觉得他们的时间够不够？

（3）为什么白琳说李信文安排日程非常有经验？

（4）白琳现在有男朋友没有？

（5）在上海和深圳的时候，美国代表计划做什么？

（6）史强生为什么尤其希望去深圳？

（7）在北京的时候，除了洽谈业务以外，美国代表还要去哪些地方？

（8）李信文修改了日程安排。现在美国代表在北京待几天？在上海和深圳待几天？

（9）李先生计划什么时候请美国客人品尝北京烤鸭？

（10）为什么去年白琳胖了十磅？

_____

2. 思考与讨论。Points for Discussion.

在安排、接待来洽谈生意的客人时，中国人有哪些习惯？在你们国家（文化）里也有这样的习惯吗？请列出三到五个相同和不同的习惯，跟你的同学进行讨论。

When it comes to receiving business associates, what do Chinese usually do? Are there similar practices in your culture? Please list three or more observations and discuss with your class.

这一课的阅读短文说，"游览和赴宴都是中国人日程安排中少不了的内容""请客吃饭有助于建立关系、发展友谊"。你同意这种说法吗？中国人喜欢这样做，你觉得还有别的原因吗？（*可以参考本课附录1的"日程表"）

In the Reading Passage, it says "sight-seeing and banquets are both an indispensable part of Chinese itinerary arrangements" and "treating people to meals is conducive to establishing relationships and developing friendships". Do you agree with these opinions? Is there any other reason that you think may cause Chinese people to do this? (You may refer to this lesson's appendix #1 "Itinerary".)

3. 小任务。Tasks.

Ⓐ 你正在计划下个月去中国的商务旅行，打算把你的日程计划事先发给中国的接待单位。请用中文写出你在中国的日程计划。例如，到达中国的时间，你要去的城市，逗留的时间，你打算参观、考察的工厂和公司，你计划跟哪些人见面，洽谈什么问题等等。请尽可能用本课的生词和句型。

You are going to China on a business trip next month, and you want to send your tentative plan to your host organization in China. Write a paragraph about your "日程安排" in Chinese. You might want to include the date that you will arrive at China, what cities you would like to visit, how long you want to stay in a particular place, what other companies and factories you want to see, who you would like to meet and what kind of business matters you would like to take care of while you're there, and so on. Use new vocabularies and patterns of this lesson whenever possible.

Ⓑ 中国有很多有意思的地方。请你介绍一个你知道的或者是听说过的地方。你可以参考本课附录里的旅游地图。

There are many interesting places in China. Can you tell one of those places that you may have heard or you have been to? You may use the map in the lesson's appendix as a reference.

4. 快速复习。Quick review.

A 阅读下面的短文，复习学过的词汇和句型。
Read the following text and review vocabularies and sentence patterns that you have learned.

今天中美双方的正式见面进行得很顺利。王总经理代表东方进出口公司对美方代表表示了欢迎。史强生先生代表美国国际贸易公司向中方说明了这次访问的目的。这次美国代表打算在中国逗留八天。他们不但要跟东方公司洽谈新订单和签订代理合同，而且想去上海和深圳考察投资环境。

见面以后，史先生、白小姐和李信文先生讨论了他们的日程安排。他们计划先在北京待四天，再去上海和深圳。李先生为他们在北京安排了很多活动。除了洽谈业务以外，他们还要参观几家工厂、看表演、游览故宫和长城。李先生告诉他们，如果有时间的话，服装厂的钱厂长、玩具厂的陈厂长都想请他们一起吃饭。李先生自己打算请他们品尝北京烤鸭。史先生和白琳知道，无论是来中国出差还是私人访问，游览和赴宴都是少不了的活动。不过，每天都得参加宴会还是让他们觉得有一点儿不习惯。白琳对李先生说："去年我听了您的安排，结果每天都有人请我吃饭。最后不但胖了十磅，而且连男朋友也吹了！"史先生知道白琳早就跟她的男朋友分开了。现在听见白琳把这件事说成是李先生的错，史先生笑了。他告诉李先生别担心，白琳是在开玩笑呢！李先生也笑了。他说，如果怕胖的话，那就多吃一些有助于健康的东西。不过李先生又说："你们到了北京，北京烤鸭当然应该吃。今天晚上我就请你们去尝一尝！"史强生和白琳都笑了。他们想，李先生这么客气，有谁还能说不去呢？

B 问答 Q & A：

（1）史先生、白小姐这次访问中国的目的是什么？

（2）今天双方代表见面以后谈了一些什么？

（3）李先生为他们在北京安排了哪些活动？

（4）史先生和白小姐对什么有一点儿不习惯？

（5）为什么史强生说白琳是开玩笑？

（6）今天晚上李先生要请史先生和白小姐去哪儿？他们愿意去吗？为什么？

日程安排 Itinerary Arrangements 4

（四）附录　Appendix

1. 日程表　Itinerary

AA 贸易代表团访华日程表

日期	时间	活动安排	备注
1月2日（星期四）	10:00	到达北京首都机场	公司××副总经理前往接机
	11:00	入住北京饭店	
	12:00–13:30	午餐	饭店三楼301包间
	14:00–14:30	会见公司××总经理	
	14:30–16:00	与市场部会谈	
	18:30–20:00	欢迎宴会	全聚德烤鸭店
1月3日（星期五）	9:30–12:00	继续与市场部会谈	
	12:00–13:00	工作午餐	
	13:00–16:00	参观京华纺织厂	市场部主任××陪同
	18:00	晚餐	饭店一楼餐厅
	19:00–21:00	观看京剧演出	
1月4日（星期六）	9:00–11:30	游览颐和园	××副总经理陪同
	12:00	北海仿膳午餐	
	14:00	参观故宫	
	19:00	告别宴会	北京饭店小宴会厅
1月5日（星期日）	10:00	离开北京	市场部主任××送往机场

2. 中国旅游地图 China Travel Map

中国地图

5 出席宴会
Attending a Banquet

王国安总经理代表东方进出口公司举行宴会,欢迎史强生先生和白琳小姐。外贸局的马局长也出席了宴会。史强生和白琳都觉得宴会非常丰盛。

(一) 对 话 Dialogue

1. 请坐,请坐,请上座 Please Take the Seats of Honor

(在餐厅)

王国安:史先生、白小姐,你们到了!请进,请进!

史强生:谢谢!

白　琳:这家餐厅布置得可真漂亮!

张　红:是啊,这是北京最有名的饭店之一,大家都喜欢到这儿来。

王国安:我来为你们介绍一下儿。 这位是外贸局的马局长,这位是美国国际贸易公司的史先生,这位是白小姐。

89

马局长：欢迎，欢迎！欢迎两位来中国！（握手）这两天辛苦了吧！

史强生：还好，不太累。虽然有一点儿时差，但是昨天休息得很好。王总为我们安排得非常周到。

王国安：各位请入席吧！史先生、白小姐，你们是客人，请坐这儿。这儿是上座。马局长，您请坐这儿！

马局长：你是主人，你应该陪客人坐一块儿呀！

王国安：不，不，不，您是领导，应该和贵宾坐一起。我坐您旁边。来，来，来，大家都请随便坐吧！

课文英译

2. 干杯，干杯！Cheers!

王国安：今天晚上是为史先生、白小姐接风。大家先喝一点儿酒，怎么样？史先生，您要茅台酒还是红葡萄酒？

史强生：我听说茅台酒非常有名，我要茅台酒吧。

王国安：白小姐，您呢？

白　琳：我不太会喝酒，我喝葡萄酒吧。

王国安：孔子说过："有朋自远方来，不亦乐乎？"来，为欢迎史先生和白小姐，干杯！（大家干杯）

马局长：史先生，请吃菜。这些都是冷盘，等会儿还有大菜和汤。来，尝尝这个！（用公筷给史强生夹菜）

史强生：谢谢，谢谢！我自己来吧。

（服务员上菜）

张　红：今天的菜都是这家饭店的特色菜。白小姐，你尝尝。喜欢吗？

白　琳：嗯，很好吃！

张　红：既然好吃，就多吃一些！你再尝尝这个。

白　琳：（笑）谢谢。桌子上这么多菜，我都吃不过来了！

史强生：王先生，我敬您一杯，感谢您和各位的热情招待！

王国安：好，我们一起干一杯。预祝我们的合作圆满成功！

出席宴会
Attending a Banquet 5

词汇（一） Vocabulary (1)

1.	出席	chūxí	to attend; be present (at a banquet, etc.)
2.	举行	jǔxíng	to hold (a meeting, etc.)
3.	局长	júzhǎng	director (of a government office or bureau)
4.	布置	bùzhì	to decorate; to arrange
5.	之一	zhīyī	one of...
6.	时差	shíchā	time difference; jet lag
7.	入席	rù xí	to take one's seat (at a ceremony, etc.)
8.	上座	shàngzuò	the seat of honor
9.	陪	péi	to accompany; to keep sb. company
10.	领导	lǐngdǎo	leader; leadership
11.	贵宾	guìbīn	honored/distinguished guest
12.	随便	suíbiàn	as you like; do as one pleases
13.	干杯	gān bēi	to drink a toast; Cheers!; Bottoms up!
14.	接风	jiēfēng	to give a welcome reception for visitors from afar
15.	葡萄酒	pútaojiǔ	wine
16.	有朋自远方来，不亦乐乎	yǒu péng zì yuǎnfāng lái, bú yì lè hū	Isn't it a joy to have friends coming from distant places?
17.	冷盘	lěngpán	cold dish; hors d'oeuvres
18.	大菜	dàcài	main dish
19.	尝	cháng	to taste
20.	公筷	gōngkuài	serving-chopsticks; chopsticks for serving food
	筷子	kuàizi	chopsticks

21.	夹菜	jiā cài	to pick up food with chopsticks
22.	上菜	shàng cài	to serve (food); to place dishes on the table
23.	特色菜	tèsècài	special dish; chef's special
24.	嗯	ǹg	"mmm" (express an agreement or satisfaction)
25.	既然	jìrán	since; given the fact that
26.	敬	jìng	to offer politely
27.	招待	zhāodài	to receive/entertain (guests); reception
28.	预祝	yùzhù	to congratulate beforehand
29.	圆满	yuánmǎn	satisfactory; satisfactorily
30.	成功	chénggōng	succeed; success; successful

专有名词 / 特殊名词 Proper Nouns / Special Nouns

1.	外贸局	wàimàojú	Foreign Trade Bureau
2.	茅台酒	Máotái Jiǔ	Maotai (liquor)
3.	孔子	Kǒngzǐ	Confucius

句型（一）　Sentence Patterns (1)

1. ……之一　　one of...

例：❶ 这是北京最有名的饭店之一。
　　❷ 我们公司是中国有名的外贸公司之一。

2. 虽然……但是/可是……　　although... but/however...

例：❶ 虽然有一点儿时差，但是昨天休息得很好。
　　❷ 这家旅馆虽然很贵，可是服务非常好。

3. 既然……就……　　given the fact that/since... then...

例：❶ 既然好吃，就多吃一些！
　　❷ 既然累了，你就休息休息吧。

4. 这么多……（我/sb.）都 V. 不过来了
there are so many... that one cannot V. all of them

例：❶ 这么多菜，我都吃不过来了！
　　❷ 买了这么多东西，我们都拿不过来了！

（二）阅读短文 Reading Passage

课文英译

中国人的宴会
Chinese Banquets

中国菜闻名世界，"吃在中国"自然也是一件非常重要的事。中国人的宴会总是非常丰盛。据说著名的满汉全席有一百多道菜。就是普通的宴会，也有十多道菜。在宴会上，贵宾和主人被安排在上座。一般来说，面对着门或入口的座位是上座。宴会当然少不了酒。"干杯"的意思是喝完你杯子里的酒。不过，如果你不想马上就醉，最好不要把酒一口气喝下去。因为中国人习惯先喝酒、吃菜，再吃饭、喝汤，所以上菜的次序是先上冷盘，再上热炒和大菜，最后是米饭、汤和甜点。老一辈的中国人还有一个习惯，就是主人应该给客人夹菜。这既代表真诚，又说明主人好客。如果你不习惯这种做法，你可以对主人说："谢谢，让我自己来。"

词汇（二） Vocabulary (2)

#			
1.	闻名	wénmíng	famous; well-known
2.	自然	zìrán	of course; naturally
3.	据说	jùshuō	it is said...
4.	道	dào	a measure word for dishes; courses
5.	普通	pǔtōng	ordinary; common; average
6.	面对	miànduì	to face
7.	入口	rùkǒu	entrance
8.	座位	zuòwèi	seat
9.	醉	zuì	drunk
10.	一口气	yìkǒuqì	in one breath; at one go; without a break; in one stretch
11.	次序	cìxù	order; sequence
12.	热炒	rèchǎo	a fried dish (stir-fried, etc.)
13.	甜点	tiándiǎn	dessert
14.	老一辈	lǎoyíbèi	older generation
15.	真诚	zhēnchéng	sincerity; sincere
16.	好客	hàokè	hospitable

专有名词 / 特殊名词 Proper Nouns / Special Nouns

#			
1.	满汉全席	Mǎn-Hàn Quánxí	the complete Manchu and Chinese banquet

句型（二） Sentence Patterns (2)

1. 据说……   it is said...; according to (sb. / media) said

例：① 据说著名的满汉全席有一百多道菜。
    ② 据王总说，美国贸易代表团明天要来我们公司参观。

2. 就是……也……   even (if)...

例：① 在中国，就是普通的宴会，也有十多道菜。
    ② 就是你很忙，也应该给他打一个电话。

3. 把 Obj. 一口气 V. + Complement   do sth. at one go/at a stretch

例：① 你最好不要把酒一口气喝下去。
    ② 我们把这些事一口气做完了再休息，好不好？

4. 先……，再……，最后……   first..., then..., lastly...

例：① 中国人习惯先喝酒、吃菜，再吃饭，最后喝汤。
    ② 明天的日程安排是先参观工厂，再参加宴会，最后看电影。

出席宴会 Attending a Banquet 5

（三）练习与活动　Exercises & Activities

I. 词汇练习　Vocabulary Exercises

1. 字谜。Crossword puzzle.

请根据下面的提示，猜一猜是哪个生词，把它的拼音填进下面的空格里，在旁边写出汉字，最后找出谜底。

Read each clue first, and then fill in the boxes with *pinyin* of the word you made a guess. You may write the characters next to each clue. Once you fill out all the boxes, find out what "the wonder word" is.

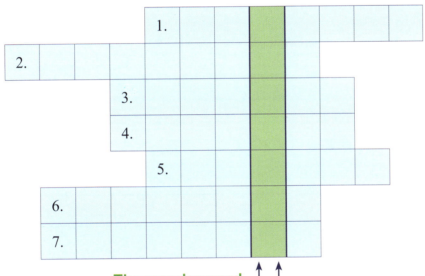

The wonder word

* 提示 (Clues):　　　　　　　　　　　　　　　　　　　　　　　　　汉字

（1）一家饭馆自己的、专门的菜　→

（2）请客吃饭的时候最好的最重要的座位　→

（3）中国人用这个东西吃饭　→

（4）最重要的客人　→

（5）两个地方的时间不一样　→

（6）结果很好、很成功　→

（7）请远方来的客人吃饭　→

97

2. 写出本课中跟参加宴会有关的词汇。
Write down any words and expressions in this lesson's vocabulary list associated with eating, drinking and attending a dinner party.

_____

_____

3. 什么是"接风"？中国人什么时候"接风"？
What is the meaning of "接风"? In what situations do Chinese people need to "接风"?

_____

4. 用中文解释以下词汇的意思，然后造句。
Use Chinese to explain the meaning of the following words, then make a sentence.

例：频繁："很多很多次"的意思。

李经理频繁地给对方打电话，总算把事情安排好了。

（1）时差：_____

_____

（2）上座：_____

_____

（3）贵宾：_____

_____

（4）入席：_____

_____

（5）圆满：_____

_____

（6）入口：_____

_____

（7）好客：_____

_____

（8）闻名：_____

_____

（9）真诚：_____

_____

（10）老一辈：_____

_____

II. 句型练习（一） Sentence Pattern Exercises (1)

1. 🎧007 用"……之一"告诉你朋友下面的事。
   Use "……之一" to make sentences about the followings.

   （1）一个中国最有名的菜
   _____

   （2）一家最好的中国旅馆
   _____

   （3）一个最重要的中国节日
   _____

   （4）一家中国（或者世界）闻名的大公司
   _____

2. 🎧008 用"虽然……但是……"礼貌地拒绝以下的邀请。
   Use "虽然……但是……" to decline an offer or invitation in the following situations, but please be polite.

   （1）主人请你喝有名的中国酒。你说：
   _____

（2）主人请你再多吃一点儿饭店的特色菜。你说：
_____

（3）开了一天的会以后，主人想请你参观他的工厂。你说：
_____

（4）你到中国洽谈生意。有一家中国公司的总裁要给你接风，可是你不想跟这家公司做生意。所以你（客气地）说：
_____

3. **用"既然……就……"完成下面的句子。**
   Complete the following sentences by using "既然…… 就……".

   （1）既然你觉得有时差，_____

   （2）既然时间很紧，_____

   （3）既然您是贵宾，_____

   （4）既然大家都是老朋友，_____

   （5）既然这种产品这么有名，_____

   （6）既然我们公司请你吃了饭，又游览了长城，_____

4. **用"这么多……（我/sb.）都 V. 不过来了"完成下面的句子。**
   Complete the following sentences by using "这么多……（我/sb.）都 V. 不过来了".

   （1）这么多工作，我都 _____

   （2）这么多电话，白小姐都 _____

   （3）这么多问题，李经理都 _____

   （4）这么多宴会，马局长都 _____

   （5）这么多货样，史先生都 _____

III. 句型练习（二） Sentence Pattern Exercises (2)

1. 用"据说"回答下面的问题。
   Answer the following questions by using the pattern of "据说".

   （1）请问有哪些外国大公司在中国做生意？

   （2）除了长城以外，外国人还喜欢去哪些地方游览？

   （3）你听说过满汉全席吗？你知道满汉全席有多少道菜吗？

   （4）你知道中国宴会的上菜次序吗？

   （5）中国人请客吃饭的时候，有哪些习惯？

2. "就是……也……"和第三课学过的"即使……也……"都是很常用的句型。它们的意思和用法差不多。请用"就是……也……"改写下面的句子。
   Both "就是……也……" and "即使……也……" (*see it in Lesson 3) are very common sentence patterns in Chinese. Their meanings and usages are exactly same. Please rewrite the following sentences by using the pattern of "就是……也……".

   （1）茅台酒非常有名，即使在美国也有很多人知道。

   （2）即使我不太会喝酒，也一定要尝尝。

   （3）这个月王总非常忙，星期六也常常在工作。

   （4）明天的洽谈很重要，你有没有时差都一定得参加。

3. 用"把 Obj. 一口气 V. + Complement"完成下面的句子。
Use the pattern of "把 Obj. 一口气 V. + Complement" to accomplish the following tasks.

（1）钱厂长非常饿。他把 ＿＿＿＿＿＿＿＿＿＿＿＿ 一口气（都）吃完了。

（2）白小姐醉了。因为她把 ＿＿＿＿＿＿＿＿＿＿＿＿ 一口气（都）喝下去了！

（3）今天的会谈很顺利。双方把 ＿＿＿＿＿＿＿＿＿＿ 一口气（都）安排好了。

（4）李经理今天很高兴。因为他把 ＿＿＿＿＿＿＿＿＿ 一口气（都）做好了。

4. 🎧011 用"先……，再……，最后……"回答下面的问题。
Use the pattern of "先……，再……，最后……" to answer the following questions.

（1）如果你去中国旅行或者做生意，你打算怎么安排你的日程？
＿＿＿＿＿＿＿＿＿＿＿＿＿＿＿＿＿＿＿＿＿＿＿＿＿＿＿＿＿＿

（2）去中国以前，你有哪些事需要准备？
＿＿＿＿＿＿＿＿＿＿＿＿＿＿＿＿＿＿＿＿＿＿＿＿＿＿＿＿＿＿

（3）明天史先生要和王总经理会谈。他们要谈些什么？
＿＿＿＿＿＿＿＿＿＿＿＿＿＿＿＿＿＿＿＿＿＿＿＿＿＿＿＿＿＿

（4）在你们国家，宴会的上菜次序是什么？
＿＿＿＿＿＿＿＿＿＿＿＿＿＿＿＿＿＿＿＿＿＿＿＿＿＿＿＿＿＿

IV. 阅读、讨论和其他活动　Reading, Discussion and Other Activities

1. 🎧012 根据课文对话回答问题。
Answer the following questions according to the dialogues in this lesson.

（1）哪些人参加了宴会？
＿＿＿＿＿＿＿＿＿＿＿＿＿＿＿＿＿＿＿＿＿＿＿＿＿＿＿＿＿＿

（2）谁是这次宴会的主人？谁是主人的贵宾？
＿＿＿＿＿＿＿＿＿＿＿＿＿＿＿＿＿＿＿＿＿＿＿＿＿＿＿＿＿＿

（3）这家饭店怎么样？
＿＿＿＿＿＿＿＿＿＿＿＿＿＿＿＿＿＿＿＿＿＿＿＿＿＿＿＿＿＿

（4）王总请史先生和白小姐坐在什么地方？
_____

（5）马局长是谁？他坐在哪儿？为什么？
_____

（6）白小姐喝了茅台酒没有？为什么？
_____

（7）为什么马局长要给客人夹菜？
_____

（8）王总为什么举行这个宴会？
_____

2. 在宴会上，王总引用了孔子的话"有朋自远方来，不亦乐乎"。你还知道孔子说过的什么话吗？如果你知道，请跟你的同学分享。

During the banquet, President Wang quoted Confucius' words *"Isn't it a joy to have friends coming from distant places?"* Do you know any other quotations from Confucius? Please share with your classmates if you know.

_____

3. 你正在一家中国饭馆请美国客人吃饭。你的客人告诉你他非常喜欢中国菜。你按照中国人请客的习惯，给客人夹菜、敬酒。请写一个小对话。试着把下面列出的句型用在对话里。

You are entertaining your American client at a Chinese restaurant and your client just told you that he/she really likes Chinese food. As a host, naturally you have to make sure he/she has plenty of food to eat. Use some of the following patterns to write a short dialogue between you and your client. Make sure that you are a good host and that your client knows how to respond appropriately.

既然……就……　　先……，再……，最后……　　据说　　都 V.不过来了

_____
_____
_____

4. 小任务。Tasks.

A 李先生和白琳小姐是老朋友了。去年夏天在北京他们合作得很愉快。这次白琳跟她的老板史强生先生一起到中国来，李先生想请他们在白琳最喜欢的全家福饭馆吃饭。李先生还邀请了公共关系部主任张红女士。全家福饭馆的菜单在本课的附录里。请你用这个菜单，帮李先生安排一桌500元左右的晚餐。

Mr. Li and Miss Lynn Petty are old friends. Last summer they had a pleasant experience working together. This time Miss Lynn Petty and her boss, Mr. Johnson Smith, have come to China. Mr. Li invites them to dinner at Miss Lynn Petty's favorite restaurant Quanjiafu. Mr. Li also invites Ms. Zhang Hong, the director of Public Relations, to join them. Please see the menu of Quanjiafu Restaurant in Lesson 5's Appendixes. Could you use this menu to plan a dinner at a price about 500 *yuan* for Mr. Li?

B 根据本课的内容和你自己的经验，比较中国宴会和美国（或者别的国家）宴会的各自特点。例如，宴会的礼节、习惯、上菜的次序等等。

Based on this lesson's text and your own experience and knowledge, give a presentation comparing a typical Chinese banquet and a typical American (or another country's) banquet. You presentation may include, but is not limited to, the etiquette and convention at a formal banquet, the general sequences for serving dishes, etc.

5. 快速复习。Quick review.

A 阅读下面的短文，复习学过的词汇和句型。

Read the following text and review vocabularies and sentence patterns that you have learned.

史先生和白小姐到达北京已经两天了。他们住在长城酒店。长城酒店是一家五星级酒店，服务很周到，设施也很完备，房间布置得非常漂亮。尤其是酒店的互联网服务，客人在自己的房间就可以免费上网，又快又方便。因为吃得好、睡得好，史先生和白小姐都觉得已经没有时差了。

今天上午，史先生、白小姐跟东方进出口公司的王国安总经理正式见了面。下午，他们跟东方公司李信文副总经理讨论了日程安排。李副总告诉他们，他已经跟服装厂、玩具厂的主管说好了去参观的事。他也联系了上海的一家高新科技公司和深圳的一家创业公司，安排好了去参观、考察的事情。晚上，王总经理在当地一家著名的饭店为他们接风。外贸局的领导马局长也参加了宴会。王总请他们喝中国的茅台酒。他还用了孔子说过的一句话欢迎史先生和白小姐。史先生知道茅台酒是中国最有名的酒，可是他也知道明天有很重要的洽谈，所以他只喝了一小杯。

B 问答 Q & A：

（1）史先生、白小姐到北京多久了？他们住在哪儿？

（2）这家旅馆怎么样？

（3）他们最喜欢这家旅馆的什么服务？

（4）史先生和白小姐还有时差吗？为什么？

（5）今天上午、下午和晚上都有什么活动？

（6）美国客人打算参观考察的地方安排好了吗？他们会去哪些地方？

（7）马局长是谁？

（8）在宴会上，王总用了一句孔子的话欢迎美国客人。你还记得是哪一句话吗？

（9）茅台酒是中国最有名的酒，可是为什么史先生只喝了一小杯？

（四）附录　Appendix

菜单实例 Sample Menu

全家福饭馆菜单

冷盘

1.凉拌黄瓜	10.00	2.凉拌海蜇	20.00
3.茶叶卤蛋	15.00	4.油炸花生	10.00
5.豆腐拌皮蛋	15.00	6.金陵鸭肫	30.00
7.五香牛肉	35.00	8.四色拼盘	35.00

水产、海鲜类

1.松子鱼	45.00	2.糖醋鱼	40.00
3.三鲜海参	70.00	4.椒盐虾	50.00
5.腰果虾仁	55.00	6.全家福烩海鲜	70.00
7.酱爆田鸡	60.00	8.红烧甲鱼	时价
9.清蒸桂鱼	时价	10.滑炒鲈鱼	时价
11.姜葱河蟹	时价	12.基围虾	时价

禽蛋类

1.辣子鸡丁	30.00	2.腰果鸡丁	30.00
3.炒鸡杂	25.00	4.三杯鸡	25.00
5.咖喱鸡片	30.00	6.宫保鸡丁	30.00
7.时素炒蛋	25.00	8.全家福涨蛋	25.00
9.香酥鸭	70.00	10.北京烤鸭	70.00

全家福饭馆菜单

煲仔类

1.什锦豆腐煲	30.00	2.香辣牛筋煲	35.00
3.冬笋腐竹煲	45.00	4.全家福海鲜煲	50.00

豆腐、蔬菜类

1.三鲜豆腐	30.00	2.家常豆腐	25.00
3.麻婆豆腐	25.00	4.松仁玉米	35.00
5.蘑菇菜心	35.00	6.肉末雪菜	30.00
7.素什锦	30.00	8.腰果西芹	45.00

猪、牛肉类

1.红烧肉	50.00	2.狮子头	45.00
3.红烧牛腩	45.00	4.炒腰花	35.00
5.回锅肉	45.00	6.木樨肉	40.00
7.梅菜扣肉	45.00	8.鱼香肉丝	40.00
9.糖醋排骨	45.00	10.咕老肉	45.00

汤菜类

1.蛋花汤	15.00	2.酸辣汤	15.00
3.三鲜汤	15.00	4.肉丝汤	15.00
5.酸辣鱼片汤	25.00	6.草菇鸡丝汤	25.00

全家福饭馆菜单

甜点类

1.拔丝苹果	25.00	2.脆皮香蕉	20.00
3.珍珠荔枝	30.00	4.八宝粥	30.00
5.玉米羹	15.00	6.银耳汤	30.00

主食

1.扬州炒饭	20.00	2.水饺（6个）	20.00
3.蒸饺（4个）	20.00	4.汤包（8个）	25.00
5.小笼包（4个）	15.00	6.炒面	20.00
7.米饭（1碗）	5.00	8.馒头（1个）	3.00

汽水、果汁饮料

1.桔子汁	15.00	2.鲜橙汁	15.00
3.椰子汁	15.00	4.柠檬汁	15.00
5.矿泉水	8.00	6.健力宝	8.00
7.可口可乐	12.00	8.百事可乐	12.00
9.雪碧	12.00	10.七喜	12.00

酒类

1.青岛啤酒（瓶）	15.00	2.百威啤酒（瓶）	15.00
3.红葡萄酒（瓶）	110.00	4.白葡萄酒（瓶）	110.00
5.二锅头（瓶）	60.00	6.竹叶青（瓶）	198.00
7.五粮液（瓶）	298.00	8.茅台酒（瓶）	498.00

（原始材料由中国江西财经大学经济文化传播系提供，有删改）

6 初步洽谈
Preliminary Negotiations

今天中美两家公司的代表要举行初步洽谈。东方进出口公司为这次洽谈做了很多准备。他们首先请美方看了产品的视频介绍，接着展示了产品货样。史强生和白琳对几款新设计特别感兴趣。

（一）对 话 Dialogue

1. 介绍产品 Introducing Products

（在会议室）

王国安： 史先生、白小姐，刚才我们一起看了产品视频。接下来由李经理向两位具体介绍产品和价格的情况，你们看怎么样？

史强生： 好啊，我们来的目的就是要谈生意的。我很想早点儿知道贵公司今年可以提供哪些东西。

李信文：这是我们今年的产品目录。请两位过目。

史强生：李先生，这些都是今年的新设计吗？

李信文：百分之八十都是新设计，只有列在最后的是我们保留的传统产品。我还带来了一些货样，也请你们看一看。（拿货样）

白　琳：嗯，真漂亮！李先生，我非常喜欢这几款设计，尤其是这件毛衣，颜色、式样都很好。

李信文：（笑）这件吗？这件是听了您上次的建议设计的。白小姐，您忘了吗？

白　琳：（笑）是吗？这么说，你准备怎么谢我呢？

2. 询问价格 Inquiring Prices

史强生：王总，贵公司今年推出的产品很有吸引力，尤其是这些新设计。请问，在目录上列出的价格是零售价还是批发价？

王国安：目录上的价格都是零售价。批发价要低百分之十五到百分之二十五。另外，部分新产品有特别的促销价。

白　琳：李先生，我注意到有些产品在目录上没有列出价格。您可以告诉我它们的价格吗？

李信文：没有列出价格的都是试销品。（指着目录）像这条牛仔裤，这几款毛衣都是厂家试生产的。如果贵公司感兴趣，价格可以参照同类产品目前的市场价另议。

史强生：按照我了解到的情况，贵公司西装的价格好像比其他几家公司的同类产品高一些。这是为什么？

李信文：我想我们的价格稍高跟产品的质量和设计有关系，尤其是这个品牌的，很受客户欢迎。您可以再比较比较。

史强生：好吧，我想把这些资料带回去，再仔细看看。

王国安：（看手表）啊，已经十二点多了。我看我们先吃中饭，然后再继续谈吧。

白　琳：（开玩笑）我同意。我的肚子已经在跟我谈判了！

词汇（一） Vocabulary (1)

1.	初步	chūbù	initial; preliminary
2.	视频	shìpín	video
3.	展示	zhǎnshì	to reveal; to show; to display; to exhibit sth.
4.	款	kuǎn	a measure word for the design of certain things (especially clothing); item/clause (in document)
5.	设计	shèjì	design; to design
6.	兴趣	xìngqù	interest；hobby
7.	由	yóu	by; through; via; from
8.	价格	jiàgé	price
9.	目录	mùlù	catalogue; list
10.	过目	guò mù	to look over (a paper/list/etc.); so as to check or approve; to go over
11.	百分之……	bǎifēnzhī……	...percent
12.	保留	bǎoliú	to retain; to continue to have
13.	传统	chuántǒng	traditional; tradition
14.	式样	shìyàng	style
15.	建议	jiànyì	suggestion; to suggest
16.	询问	xúnwèn	to ask about; to inquire
17.	推出	tuīchū	to present (to the public); to put out
18.	吸引力	xīyǐnlì	appeal
	吸引	xīyǐn	to attract; to draw
19.	零售价	língshòujià	retail price
20.	批发价	pīfājià	wholesale price
21.	促销价	cùxiāojià	sale price
22.	试销品	shìxiāopǐn	trial item/products

23.	牛仔裤	niúzǎikù	jeans
24.	厂家	chǎngjiā	manufacturer
25.	试生产	shìshēngchǎn	to manufacture on a trial basis; trial production
26.	参照	cānzhào	to refer to; to consult
27.	同类	tónglèi	the same kind; similar
28.	市场价	shìchǎngjià	market price
	市场	shìchǎng	market
29.	另议	lìngyì	be discussed/negotiated separately
30.	按照	ànzhào	according to; on the basis of
31.	西装	xīzhuāng	Western-style clothes; suit
32.	质量	zhìliàng	quality
33.	品牌	pǐnpái	brand name; trademark
34.	客户	kèhù	client; customer
35.	资料	zīliào	date; means; material
36.	仔细	zǐxì	careful(ly); attentive(ly)

句型（一） Sentence Patterns (1)

1. 对……感兴趣　　to be interested in...

    例：① 我对这些新设计特别感兴趣。
    ② 美国代表团对今年的交易会很感兴趣。

2. 由 sb. + V. + sth.　　（由 introduces the person in charge of a given task）

    例：① 今天由李经理向美国代表介绍产品和价格的情况。
    ② 明天由张小姐去酒店接你们。

3. 按照……　according to; on the basis of

例：① 按照我了解到的情况，贵公司西装的价格好像比其他几家公司的同类产品高一些。
② 按照贵公司的建议，我们保留了几种传统的设计。

4. 跟……有关系　have something to do with...; related to...

例：① 这种产品的价格跟质量和设计有关系。
② 每天都这么忙跟我们的日程安排有关系。

（二）阅读短文　Reading Passage

货比三家不吃亏
It Pays to Shop Around

课文英译

　　无论是买东西，还是做生意，价格都是买主和卖主最关心的事之一。中国有句老话，叫做"货比三家不吃亏"。意思是如果你想买东西，最好多去几家商店，比较比较它们的价钱和质量。只有这样才不会吃亏上当，才能买到又便宜又满意的好东西。

　　自从1979年实行改革开放政策以后，中国的市场经济有了很大的发展。在商品的价格、质量和品种上，顾客都有了更多的选择。市场竞争一方面带来了更多的机会，一方面也带来了更多的挑战。如果你打算到中国去做生意，一定要事先了解中国的市场行情，充分掌握有关信息。《孙子兵法》上说，"知己知彼"，才能成功。做生意也是这样。

词汇（二） Vocabulary (2)

1.	货	huò	goods; commodities
2.	吃亏	chī kuī	to suffer loss; to come to grief; to be at a disadvantage
3.	买主	mǎizhǔ	buyer
4.	卖主	màizhǔ	seller; vendor
5.	老话	lǎohuà	old saying; adage
6.	价钱	jiàqián	price
7.	只有	zhǐyǒu	only
8.	上当	shàng dàng	to be fooled/taken in
9.	自从	zìcóng	since
10.	实行	shíxíng	to implement; to put into practice; to carry out
11.	改革	gǎigé	reform; to reform
12.	开放	kāifàng	to open (to trade/to the public/etc.); to lift a ban or restriction
13.	政策	zhèngcè	policy
14.	市场经济	shìchǎng jīngjì	market economy; market-directed economy
15.	品种	pǐnzhǒng	variety; assortment; kind
16.	顾客	gùkè	customer
17.	选择	xuǎnzé	choice; to choose
18.	竞争	jìngzhēng	competition; to compete
19.	一方面	yì fāngmiàn	one side; on the one hand
20.	挑战	tiǎozhàn	challenge; to challenge
21.	行情	hángqíng	business conditions; market conditions; quotation
22.	充分	chōngfèn	full; fully
23.	有关	yǒuguān	concerning; related to; to relate; have sth. to do with
24.	信息	xìnxī	information

25. 知己知彼　zhījǐ-zhībǐ　to know one's self and know the enemy

专有名词 / 特殊名词 Proper Nouns / Special Nouns

1. 改革开放政策　Gǎigé Kāifàng Zhèngcè　the Reform and Opening-up to the Outside World policy (*first implemented in 1979)

2. 孙子兵法　Sūnzǐ Bīngfǎ　*The Art of War* by Sun Wu, ancient Chinese philosopher during the Chunqiu period (777-476 B.C.).

句型（二）Sentence Patterns (2)

1. 只有……才……　only (if) ..., (then) ...

例：① 只有这样才不会吃亏上当。
② 只有看了货样以后，我们才能做出决定。

2. 又……又……　both... and...

例：① 多去几家商店，比较比较它们的价钱，你才能买到又便宜又满意的好东西。
② 这次来中国，我们又要谈生意，又要参观考察。

3. 自从……以后　(ever) since...

例：① 自从实行改革开放政策以后，中国的市场经济有了很大的发展。
② 自从来到中国以后，史先生每天都说中文。

4. 在……上　in terms of...; as far as...

例：① 在商品的价格、质量和品种上，顾客都有了更多的选择。
② 在式样上，贵公司今年推出的新设计非常有吸引力。

115

5. 一方面……，一方面……
on the one hand..., on the other hand...; for one thing..., for another...

例：① 市场竞争一方面带来了更多的机会，一方面也带来了更多的挑战。

② 今年我们一方面保留了一些传统产品，一方面也推出了一些新设计。

（三）练习与活动　Exercises & Activities

I. 词汇练习　Vocabulary Exercises

1. 字谜。Crossword puzzle.

请根据下面的提示，猜一猜是哪个生词，把它的拼音填进下面的空格里，在旁边写出汉字，最后找出谜底。

Read each clue first, and then fill in the boxes with *pinyin* of the word you guessed. You may write the characters next to each clue. Once you fill out all the boxes, find out what "the wonder word" is.

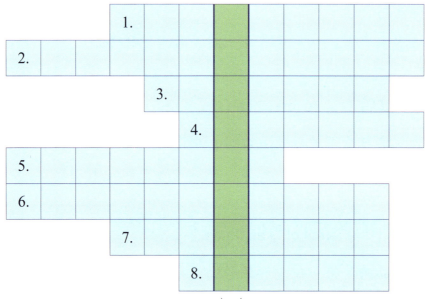

初步洽谈
Preliminary Negotiations 6

* 提示 (Clues)： 汉字

（1）西方式样的衣服 →
（2）在商店里看到的价格 →
（3）向人提出自己的看法、意见 →
（4）不放在一起讨论 →
（5）大量买/卖一种产品时的价格 →
（6）试着卖的新产品 →
（7）相同的一种 →
（8）把东西交给对方看一看或检查一下儿 →

2. 写出本课中跟价格有关的词汇。
   Write down any words and expressions in this lesson's vocabulary list associated with "price".

   （1）_____ （2）_____ （3）_____
   （4）_____ （5）_____ （6）_____

3. "货比三家不吃亏"。买东西的时候，除了比较价钱以外，你还会注意什么？请用中文写出这些词汇。
   "Compare the merchandise at three shops, and you won't come to grief." Besides comparing prices, what else do you care about when you are shopping? Please write down them in Chinese.

   （1）_____ （2）_____ （3）_____
   （4）_____ （5）_____ （6）_____

4. 反义词。Antonyms.

   （1）批发价：_____ （2）推出：_____
   （3）询问：_____ （4）传统：_____
   （5）西装：_____ （6）买主：_____

117

5. 用中文解释以下词汇的意思，然后造句。
Use Chinese to explain the meaning of the following words, then make a sentence.

例：频繁："很多很多次"的意思。

李经理频繁地给对方打电话，总算把事情安排好了。

（1）初步：_____

（2）过目：_____

（3）同类：_____

（4）另议：_____

（5）零售价：_____

（6）西装：_____

（7）吃亏：_____

（8）顾客：_____

（9）充分：_____

（10）知己知彼：_____

初步洽谈
Preliminary Negotiations 6

6. 想一想以下每组词汇在意义或用法上的不同并尝试造句。
   Distinguish the meanings or usages of the words in each group below, and then try to make a sentence for each of them.

（1）"过目"和"考察"：_____
_____

（2）"按照"和"参照"：_____
_____

（3）"首先"和"事先"：_____
_____

（4）"价格"和"价钱"：_____
_____

（5）"仔细"和"小心"：_____
_____

（6）"客户"和"顾客"：_____
_____

（7）"讨论""谈判"和"另议"：_____
_____
_____

II. 句型练习（一） Sentence Pattern Exercises (1)

1. 🎧 007 **用"对……感兴趣"回答下面的问题。**
   Answer the following questions by using the pattern "对……感兴趣".

（1）这是我们的产品目录，请过目。请问，贵公司对哪些产品感兴趣？
_____

（2）您喜欢这款新设计还是喜欢那款传统的设计？
_____

119

（3）请问，您这次来中国打算参观游览哪些地方？
_____

（4）那位美国贸易代表为什么一定要去深圳考察？
_____

2. **你正在向一个外国贸易代表团客人说明今后几天的日程安排。请用"由 sb. + V. + sth."告诉你的客人，谁会为他们介绍公司情况和介绍产品，谁会带他们参观工厂，谁会陪他们考察工业园区，谁会陪他们游览风景等等。**

   You are explaining to your guests, a foreign business delegation, about the itinerary that you made for them. Use the pattern of "由 sb. + V. + sth." to tell the details in Chinese, such as who will give an introduction about the host company and products, who will take them to see the factory, who will arrange a trip to the industrial park, who will accompany them to do sight-seeing tour, etc.

   （1）_____
   （2）_____
   （3）_____
   （4）_____

3. **用"按照"完成下面的句子。**

   Complete the following sentences by using the pattern of "按照".

   （1）按照中国宴会的习惯，_____
   （2）按照日程安排，_____
   （3）按照贵公司的建议，_____
   （4）按照我了解的市场情况，_____

4. 🎧 **用"跟……有关系"回答下面的问题。**

   Answer the following questions by using the pattern "跟……有关系".

   （1）为什么白小姐胖了十磅？
   _____

初步洽谈
Preliminary Negotiations

6

（2）为什么她跟男朋友吹了？

_____

（3）为什么王总经理这几天特别忙？

_____

（4）为什么美国公司的那位总裁先生好像不太高兴？

_____

（5）贵公司牛仔裤的批发价比市场价高了百分之十五。请问为什么？

_____

III. 句型练习（二） Sentence Pattern Exercises (2)

1. 🎧 009 用"只有……才……"回答下面的问题。
Answer the following questions by using the pattern "只有……才……".

（1）老板，我们到达北京已经三天了。哪天我们可以去游览长城？

_____

（2）选择、购买（gòumǎi / to purchase）商品的时候，怎样才能不吃亏上当？

_____

（3）在哪儿才能吃到真正好吃的北京烤鸭？

_____

（4）怎样才能提高我的中文水平？

_____

2. 🎧 010 用"又……又……"回答下面的问题。
Answer the following questions by using the pattern "又……又……".

（1）你常去哪家商店买东西？为什么？

_____

121

（2）你愿意用哪家公司生产的电脑？为什么？
　　_____

（3）如果可能的话，你喜欢住几星级宾馆？为什么？
　　_____

（4）听说上次去中国，您的日程安排得很满？
　　是啊，_____

（5）"知己知彼"这句话是什么意思？
　　_____

3. 🎧 011　**根据下面的要求，用"自从……以后"造句。**
Use the pattern "自从……以后" to accomplish the following tasks.

（1）说一说这几年手机设计的变化。
　　_____

（2）说一说一种服装式样的变化。
　　_____

（3）说一说你的国家的经济情况。
　　_____

（4）说一说你自己的变化。
　　_____

4. **你正在发布会（fābùhuì / news conference）上介绍今年你们公司的新产品。你相信你们的产品是最好的。请用"在……上"说明你们的产品和其他公司的同类产品有什么不同。（提示：你可以说一说你们产品的质量、设计、价格、材料等等）**

You are presenting this year's new products of your company at a news conference. You believe that your products are the best ones. Please use the pattern of "在……上" to tell what makes your products special by comparing with similar products made by other companies. (Hint: you may talk about the product's quality, design, price, materials etc.)

（1）_____
（2）_____

初步洽谈
Preliminary Negotiations 6

（3）_____

（4）_____

5. 🎧 012 用"一方面……一方面……"回答下面的问题。
Answer the following questions by using the pattern "一方面……一方面……".

（1）这次史先生和白小姐去中国有什么计划？
_____

（2）如果你去中国的话，你打算做什么？
_____

（3）改革开放政策给中国带来了哪些变化？
_____

（4）你觉得市场竞争的结果是什么？
_____

IV. 阅读、讨论和其他活动　Reading, Discussion and Other Activities

1. 🎧 013 根据课文对话回答问题。
Answer the following questions according to the dialogues in this lesson.

（1）今天中美两家公司的代表要做什么？
_____

（2）今年东方进出口公司的产品有多少是新设计的？
_____

（3）传统产品列在产品目录的什么地方？
_____

（4）白小姐问李先生说："你准备怎么谢我呢？"她为什么这么问？
_____

（5）美方代表对什么产品感兴趣？
_____

123

（6）零售价高还是批发价高？高多少？

（7）为什么有些产品没有列出价格？这些产品的价格怎么决定？

（8）为什么东方进出口公司的西装比较贵？

（9）白琳说："我的肚子已经在跟我谈判了。"她的意思是什么？

2. **根据阅读短文回答问题。**
   Answer the following questions based on the Reading Passage.

（1）"货比三家不吃亏"这句话是什么意思？你买东西的时候这样做过吗？为什么？

（2）哪本书里说过"知己知彼"这句话？是谁说的？这句话跟做生意有什么关系？

3. **小任务。** Tasks.

A 你是一家大商场（shāngchǎng / department store）的业务代表。你的老板要你向几家公司询问一下儿年轻人服装（例如衬衫、裙子、外套、牛仔裤、毛衣、大衣等等）的批发价。请按照下面的要求写一个对话或者一篇小报告。（可以上网找出信息或者参考本课的附录）

（1）你看了几家公司的产品目录和资料，也上网看了他们的产品介绍。你对其中一家公司的产品很感兴趣。所以，你现在给他们打电话……

（2）你已经得到了你需要的信息。现在你向老板报告询问价格的结果。你建议你的老板买哪家的产品。

You are a representative of a major department store. Your boss has asked you to check the wholesale prices of youth shirts, skirts, jackets, jeans, sweaters and overcoats with several different companies. Please write a dialogue or a short memorandum based on instructions below. You may go online to find the information or you may refer to the appendix in this lesson.

（1）You have checked their catalogues and web sites. Now you are calling a company whose products you are interested in;

（2）You have accomplished your investigation and research. Now you report to your boss the result and present your proposal of purchasing.

4. 快速复习。**Quick review.**

A 阅读下面的短文，复习学过的词汇和句型。
Read the following text and review vocabularies and sentence patterns that you have learned.

参加了昨天晚上的欢迎宴会以后，史先生和白小姐回到酒店休息。虽然比较累，但是史先生睡得不太好。他觉得他的时差问题好像又回来了。按照日程安排，今天中美双方代表要举行初步商务洽谈。史先生和白小姐已经为今天的洽谈做了很多准备。上午八点半，东方进出口公司公关部的张红主任开车来酒店接史先生和白小姐。从酒店到东方公司有点儿远，不过今天路上车不多，所以很快就到了。

中方的王国安总经理和李信文副总经理已经在公司会议室等他们了。双方握手、问好以后，王总先请美国客人看了一个产品视频。史先生觉得这个视频做得很漂亮，可是不够具体。李副总拿出了两本服装产品目录，客气地说："这是我们今年的产品目录，请二位过目。"他告诉史先生和白小姐："列在目录前面的都是今年的新产品，列在最后几页的是保留的传统产品。目录上的价格都是零售价。批发价要低百分之二十左右。"李副总又拿出了一些货样请他们看一看。美方代表对其中一些新设计的服装产品特别感兴趣。他们觉得这几款服装的式样、颜色都非常好。如果在美国市场上推出，一定很有吸引力。不过，他们也有一些问题要问。

白小姐注意到有几款很漂亮的产品没有列出价格。史先生想知道为什么西装的价格比别的公司的高。李副总告诉他们，那些没有列出价格的都是试销品。如果美方打算要，价格可以参照同类产品的市场价另议。另外，这个品牌的西装是他们传统的出口产品，质量和设计都特别好，所以价格也高一点儿。

到午饭的时间了，双方决定吃完饭以后再继续洽谈。

B 问答 Q & A:

（1）史先生今天觉得还有时差吗？为什么？
_____

（2）从酒店到东方公司，路上顺利吗？
_____

（3）今天的洽谈是双方第几次商务洽谈？
_____

（4）他们今天的洽谈在什么地方举行？
_____

（5）史先生看了产品视频以后觉得怎么样？
　　_____

（6）美方代表看的是什么产品目录？
　　_____

（7）目录上有没有列出产品的批发价？
　　_____

（8）批发价比零售价低多少？
　　_____

（9）美方为什么对其中几款新设计特别感兴趣？
　　_____

（10）看了产品目录和货样以后，美方有什么问题吗？
　　_____

（11）试销品的价格可以怎样决定？
　　_____

（12）这个品牌的西装为什么比较贵？
　　_____

（13）到吃午饭的时候，他们谈完了没有？
　　_____

（四）附录 Appendix

1. 产品目录 Product Catalogue

东风服装进出口公司服装产品目录

编号	品名	生产厂家	品牌	价格（元）／打
01	T恤衫	南海迪泰针织毛衫有限公司	泰迪	600.00
02	圆领条纹衫	南海迪泰针织毛衫有限公司	泰迪	960.00
03	女衬衫	广东汕头纺织品进出口公司	金花	1440.00
04	男衬衫	广东汕头纺织品进出口公司	金花	1800.00
05	针织羊毛衫	上海爱达针织制衣公司	爱达	2400.00
06	纯羊毛休闲衫	上海爱达针织制衣公司	爱达	3000.00
07	女式大衣	长城四季时装有限公司	四季	5400.00
08	男式大衣	长城四季时装有限公司	四季	6000.00
09	羊绒大衣	内蒙古雪花绒毛制品有限公司	雪绒	9600.00

2. 时装设计 Fashion Design

7 参观工厂
Visiting a Factory

中美双方的第一次洽谈结束以后,张红陪史强生和白琳去参观了一家玩具工厂。他们公司上次订购的一批玩具就是在这儿制造的。玩具厂的管理水平和生产效率给了他们很深刻的印象。

（一）对 话 Dialogue

1. 在会客室 In the Reception Room

张　红：陈厂长，您的客人到了！

陈厂长：欢迎，欢迎！欢迎光临本厂！我来自我介绍一下儿吧。我叫陈大方，是这儿的厂长。您一定就是美国国际贸易公司的史先生了！

史强生：对，我是史强生。这位是我的助理，白琳小姐。

白　琳：您好，陈厂长！听张主任说，我们去年订购的一批玩具就是在这儿生产的，是吗？

陈厂长：对、对、对，我记得那批玩具是赶在圣诞节前交货的。史先生、白小姐，贵公司对那批产品满意吗？

史强生：非常满意。我们这次来，一是要对贵厂表示感谢，二是想亲眼看看贵厂的生产情况。

陈厂长：史先生，您太客气了！这样吧，我们先一起看一个视频，大致了解一下儿我们厂的情况，然后我再陪各位去生产区各个车间看看。张主任，您说怎么样？

张　红：行啊！（对史强生和白琳）您二位如果有什么问题，可以随时向陈厂长提出来。他在这儿已经十多年了，非常了解厂里各方面的情况。

史强生、白琳：好！

2. 在生产区 At the Production Area

课文英译

陈厂长：这儿是我们厂的组装车间。产品在这儿组装好以后，再送到成品车间通过质量检验。

白　琳：陈厂长，你们的车间不但管理得很好，而且设备也很先进啊！

陈厂长：哪里，哪里。我们去年从国外引进了这两条组装线。现在产量比两年前增加了三倍，不但成本降低了，而且质量也提高了。

史强生：这些正在组装的卡通玩具是要出口的吗？

陈厂长：对。这些玩具都是为迪士尼公司生产的。他们计划在今年秋季投放市场，所以催得很紧。

白　琳：这些玩具太可爱了！我想它们一定会很受欢迎！

史强生：陈厂长，你们的工厂给我的印象非常好。我希望今后我们能有更多的合作。

陈厂长：那太好了！我们以后多多联系！

参观工厂
Visiting a Factory

词汇（一） Vocabulary (1)

1.	订购	dìnggòu	to order (goods)
2.	批	pī	a measure word for goods; batch; lot
3.	制造	zhìzào	to make; to manufacture
4.	管理	guǎnlǐ	to manage; to run; to administer; management
5.	生产效率	shēngchǎn xiàolǜ	productivity
	效率	xiàolǜ	efficiency
6.	深刻	shēnkè	deep; profound
7.	印象	yìnxiàng	impression
8.	会客室	huìkèshì	reception room
9.	本厂	běnchǎng	one's own factory; this factory
10.	自我	zìwǒ	self; oneself
11.	记得	jìdé	to remember; to recall
12.	赶	gǎn	to rush; to hurry; to make a dash for
13.	交货	jiāo huò	to deliver goods
14.	大致	dàzhì	roughly; approximately; in general
15.	车间	chējiān	workshop
16.	提出（来）	tí chū (lái)	to pose (questions); to raise (an issue); to put forward (one's opinion)
17.	生产区	shēngchǎnqū	production area
18.	组装	zǔzhuāng	to assemble; assembly
19.	成品	chéngpǐn	finished products
20.	检验	jiǎnyàn	inspection; to inspect
21.	设备	shèbèi	equipment; facilities
22.	先进	xiānjìn	advanced; state-of-the-art
23.	国外	guówài	overseas; abroad

24.	引进	yǐnjìn	to introduce from elsewhere; to import
25.	组装线	zǔzhuāngxiàn	assembly line
26.	产量	chǎnliàng	output; yield
27.	成本	chéngběn	cost
28.	降低	jiàngdī	to reduce; to lower; to cut down
29.	卡通	kǎtōng	cartoon
30.	投放	tóufàng	to throw in; to put (sth. on the market)
31.	催	cuī	to urge; to hasten; to press
32.	可爱	kě'ài	cute; lovable

专有名词 / 特殊名词 Proper Nouns / Special Nouns

| 1. | 圣诞节 | Shèngdàn Jié | Christmas |
| 2. | 迪士尼 | Díshìní | Disney |

参观工厂
Visiting a Factory 7

句型（一） Sentence Patterns (1)

1. **A 给 B……的印象 / A 给 B 的印象 + Adj.**
   A makes...impression on B

   例：① 玩具厂的管理水平和生产效率给了他们很深刻的印象。
   ② 你们的工厂给我的印象非常好。

2. **对……满意   be satisfied with...**

   例：① 贵公司对那批产品满意吗？
   ② 客户对交货时间不太满意。

3. **赶在……前 V.   rush/hurry to V. before...**

   例：① 我记得那批玩具是赶在圣诞节前交货的。
   ② 我得赶在十点以前到（达）飞机场。

4. **一是……，二是……**
   one (of the reasons, etc.) is..., the other is...; on the one hand..., on the other hand...

   例：① 我们这次来，一是要对贵厂表示感谢，二是想亲眼看看贵厂的生产情况。
   ② 我买东西，一是要质量好，二是要便宜。

5. **A 比 B + V. + specific quantity (or rough estimation)**
   A V. + specific quantity (or rough estimation) than B

   例：①（现在的）产量比两年前增加了三倍。
   ② 今年的质量比去年提高了不少！

133

（二）阅读短文 Reading Passage

中国的企业
Chinese Enterprises

中国的企业大致可以分为国有企业、民营企业和外资企业几种。国有企业由中央政府或当地政府投资并进行管理。因为有国家的支持，国有企业在资金、原料、技术和销售上都有一定的优势，但是也有不少国有企业管理不善、长期亏损。中国的民营企业在最近二三十年里得到了迅速的发展，成为国有企业有力的竞争对手。目前，中国政府正在积极推动国有企业的改革，鼓励个人或私有企业承包、租赁、兼并或者购买那些效益不好的国有企业。在这一改革过程中，民营企业逐渐发展成国有民营和私有民营两种类型。在中国的外资企业主要包括外商独资企业和中外合资企业两种。很多世界五百强企业在中国都有投资。

中国政府的经济政策对企业有很大的影响。国有企业也好，民营企业也好，都需要按照政府的经济政策调整自己的发展计划。因为得到中国政府改革开放政策的鼓励，许多国有企业和民营企业都在积极寻求与外国企业的合作。这也是进入中国市场的一个大好机会。

参观工厂
Visiting a Factory 7

词汇（二） Vocabulary (2)

1.	企业	qǐyè	enterprise; business
2.	分为	fēnwéi	to divide (into)
3.	国有	guóyǒu	state-owned
4.	民营	mínyíng	privately-run
5.	外资企业	wàizī qǐyè	foreign-capital enterprises
	外资	wàizī	foreign investment
6.	中央	zhōngyāng	central (government, etc.)
7.	政府	zhèngfǔ	government
8.	并	bìng	and; besides; moreover
9.	支持	zhīchí	support; to support
10.	资金	zījīn	financial resources; funds
11.	原料	yuánliào	raw material
12.	销售	xiāoshòu	sales; marketing; to sell; to market
13.	优势	yōushì	advantage; superiority; dominant position
14.	不少	bùshǎo	not few; many
15.	不善	búshàn	not good; bad; not good at
16.	长期	chángqī	over a long period of time; long-term
17.	亏损	kuīsǔn	financial loss; deficit; to suffer a loss
18.	有力	yǒulì	strong; powerful
19.	对手	duìshǒu	opponent; adversary
20.	积极	jījí	positive(ly); active(ly)
21.	推动	tuīdòng	to push forward; to promote; to give impetus to; to spur
22.	鼓励	gǔlì	to encourage; to urge

135

23.	个人	gèrén	individual; oneself
24.	私有	sīyǒu	privately-owned
25.	承包	chéngbāo	to contract
26.	租赁	zūlìn	to rent; to lease; lease
27.	兼并	jiānbìng	to merge; to annex; merger
28.	购买	gòumǎi	to purchase; to buy
29.	效益	xiàoyì	beneficial result; benefit
30.	过程	guòchéng	course (of events); process
31.	逐渐	zhújiàn	gradually
32.	独资企业	dúzī qǐyè	single venture enterprise
33.	合资企业	hézī qǐyè	joint venture enterprise
34.	类型	lèixíng	type; category
35.	调整	tiáozhěng	to adjust
36.	寻求	xúnqiú	to seek; to pursue
37.	进入	jìnrù	to enter; to get into

专有名词 / 特殊名词 Proper Nouns / Special Nouns

1.	世界五百强（企业）	Shìjiè Wǔbǎi Qiáng (qǐyè)	Fortune Global 500 (companies)

句型（二） Sentence Patterns (2)

1. A 分为（/成）…… A can be categorized into...

例：① 中国的企业大致可以分为国有企业、民营企业和外资企业几种。
② 中国的宾馆分成二星、三星、四星和五星级几种。

2. A 对 B 有影响 A has an impact on B; A influences B

例：① 中国政府的经济政策对企业有很大的影响。
② 从国外引进的这条组装线对产品质量有很大的影响。

3. 在……过程中 in the process of...; during the course of...

例：① 在这一改革过程中，民营企业逐渐发展成国有民营和私有民营两种类型。
② 美方代表在谈判过程中提出了新的要求。

4. A 也好，B 也好 no matter whether A or B

例：① 国有企业也好，民营企业也好，都需要按照政府的经济政策调整自己的发展计划。
② 新设计的产品也好，传统产品也好，我们都生产。

137

（三）练习与活动　Exercises & Activities

I. 词汇练习　Vocabulary Exercises

1. 字谜。Crossword puzzle.

请根据下面的提示，猜一猜是哪个生词，把它的拼音填进下面的空格里，在旁边写出汉字，最后找出谜底。

Read each clue first, and then fill in the boxes with *pinyin* of the word you guessed. You may write the characters next to each clue. Once you fill out all the boxes, find out what "the wonder word" is.

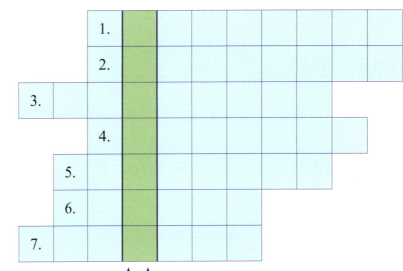

The wonder word ↑↑

* 提示 (Clues)：　　　　　　　　　　　　　　　　　汉字

（1）生产、制造产品需要花的钱　→　☐

（2）在公司跟客人见面的房间　→　☐

（3）生产、制造好了的产品　→　☐

（4）制造好了产品以后，一件一件地看它们的质量　→　☐

（5）把货交给买主　　→　　☐

（6）大概的、不需要很具体的　　→　　☐

（7）从别的地方把先进的东西介绍进来　　→　　☐

2. 组词。你可以参考总附录中的词表。
Build upon the following words. You may refer to the Vocabulary List in the General Appendix.

A 例：（具）体　　（身）体

（1）设（　　）　　设（　　）

（2）自（　　）　　自（　　）

（3）投（　　）　　投（　　）

（4）效（　　）　　效（　　）

（5）货（　　）　　（　　）货

（6）（　　）量　　（　　）量

（7）交（　　）　　交（　　）　　交（　　）

（8）本（　　）　　本（　　）　　本（　　）

（9）成（　　）　　成（　　）　　成（　　）

（10）（　　）品　　（　　）品　　（　　）品

B 例：购买　→　__购买产品__　　__购买汽车__

（1）降低　→　_____　　_____

（2）引进　→　_____　　_____

（3）提出　→　_____　　_____

（4）先进　→　_____　　_____

（5）寻求　→　_____　　_____

（6）长期　→　_____　　_____

（7）自我 → _____ _____

（8）调整 → _____ _____

（9）推动 → _____ _____

（10）效率 → _____ _____

3. 用下面括号中给出的词填空。
Fill in the blanks by using the words in the parentheses.

> 效率　制造　管理　设备

（1）这是一家 _____ 卡通玩具的工厂。工厂的 _____ 先进，产品质量好，_____ 水平和生产 _____ 都很高。

> 检验　催　车间　批　赶　成品　投放

（2）参观了组装 _____ 以后，我们又参观了 _____ 车间。陈厂长告诉我们，正在 _____ 的这 _____ 产品要 _____ 在新年前 _____ 市场，所以客户 _____ 得很紧。

> 效率　引进　进入　先进　印象　迅速
> 逐渐　寻求　亏损　管理　成本

（3）过去，因为我们公司的 _____ 不善，所以长期 _____。自从公司从 _____ 国家 _____ 最新技术以后，我们的生产 _____ 就开始提高了，_____ 也 _____ 降低了。因为我们给客户的 _____ 越来越好了，所以订单也就 _____ 增加了。最近不但有外国公司 _____ 和我们合作的机会，而且我们也成功地 _____ 了国际市场。

参观工厂
Visiting a Factory

II. 句型练习（一）　Sentence Pattern Exercises (1)

1. 用"A 给 B……的印象"或者"A 给 B 的印象 + Adj."完成句子。
   Complete the sentences by using "A 给 B……的印象" 或者 "A 给 B 的印象 + Adj.".

　　*除了可以用"很好"来形容"印象"以外，"深刻 (shēnkè / profound)""难忘 (nánwàng / unforgettable)""美好 (měihǎo / fine, beautiful)""糟糕 (zāogāo / terrible)""恶劣 (èliè / nasty, horrible)"这些词也常被用来形容"印象"。请你在完成下面的句子时，试着把它们用在句子里。

　　*In addition to using the word "很好," words like "深刻 (shēnkè / profound)" "难忘 (nánwàng / unforgettable)" "美好 (měihǎo / fine, beautiful)" "糟糕 (zāogāo / terrible)" "恶劣 (èliè / nasty, horrible)" are also used to describe one's "impression (印象)." Please use those words when you try to complete the sentences below.

（1）这家五星旅馆的服务给我的印象 _____。

　　　我打算下次来上海的时候 _____。

（2）这款新设计给美方代表的印象 _____，所以他们决定 _____。

（3）玩具厂的管理水平给了史先生 _____ 的印象。史先生真不希望 _____。

（4）新引进的组装线给了陈厂长 _____ 的印象。他 _____ _____。

2. 请用"对……满意"回答下面的问题。
   Answer the following questions by using the pattern of "对……满意".

（1）你对哪款手机产品最满意？
　　　_____

（2）总裁为什么决定让小张当经理？
　　　_____

（3）怎样才能使客户对（你的）产品满意？

_____

（4）这次到中国访问，史先生对什么满意？对什么不满意？

_____

3. 用"赶在……前 V."回答下面的问题。
   Answer the following questions by using the pattern of "赶在……前 V.".

（1）请问李经理，这份订单我最好什么时候发出去？

_____

（2）那批新款毛衣贵公司计划在什么时候投放市场？

_____

（3）这张订单上的产品我们应该什么时候交货？

_____

（4）您今天为什么这么忙？

_____

4. 根据下面的要求，用"一是……，二是……"造句。
   Use the pattern of "一是……，二是……" to accomplish the following tasks.

（1）说一说明天谈判的内容。

_____

（2）说一说为什么你们公司决定引进新的组装线。

_____

（3）说一说为什么迪士尼希望订购这家玩具厂的产品。

_____

（4）说一说他们考察那家服装厂的目的。

_____

5. 根据下面的数据，用"A 比 B + V. + specific quantity or (rough estimation)"比较说明去年和今年的生产情况。
According to the chart below, compare this year's statistics with last year's by using the pattern of "A 比 B + V. + specific quantity or (rough estimation)".

	去年	今年
成本	100,000 元 / 万件	90,000 元 / 万件
服装产量	320,000 件 / 月	640,000 件 / 月
质量	💣💣	☺☺☺
新设计	12 种	36 种

（1）_____

（2）_____

（3）_____

（4）_____

III. 句型练习（二） Sentence Pattern Exercises (2)

1. 用"分为（/成）……"回答下面的问题。
Answer the following questions by using the pattern of "分为（/成）……".

（1）请问，那家玩具厂分为哪几个车间？

_____

（2）请问，这本目录上列出的价格有哪几种？

_____

（3）一般说，中国的企业有哪几种？

_____

（4）你知道中国的宾馆有几种星级吗？

_____

2. 🎧 011 **用"A 对 B 有影响"回答下面的问题。**
Answer the following questions by using the pattern of "A 对 B 有影响".

（1）你觉得什么对产品的价格有影响？
　　_____

（2）你觉得什么对产量有影响？
　　_____

（3）你觉得什么对一家企业的效益有影响？
　　_____

（4）你觉得什么对中国的经济有影响？
　　_____

3. 用"在……过程中"完成下面的句子。你可以参考每个句子下面的提示。
Complete the following sentences by using the pattern of "在……过程中". You may refer to the "hint" under the each sentence.

（1）在昨天的洽谈过程中，双方代表讨论了 _____。
　　　　　　　　　　　　　　　　　　　　　　(The issues about cost and price)

（2）在参观玩具厂的过程中，_____。
　　　　　　　　　　　(I found out that those cute teddy bears are made here!)

（3）在产品检验过程中，_____。
　　　　　　　　　　　　　　　　　(The factory director found out that...)

（4）中国在改革开放的过程中，_____。
　　　(Many privately-run enterprises have become competitors for state-owned business)

4. 🎧 012 **用"A 也好，B 也好"回答下面的问题。请注意每句的提示。**
Answer the following questions by using the pattern of "A 也好，B 也好". Please pay attention to the hint under each sentence.

（1）您想看看样品还是参观车间？
　　_____
　　　　　　　　　　　　　　　　　　(I want to see both.)

（2）您想知道零售价还是批发价？
_____
(I want to know both)

（3）您对承包那家企业感兴趣还是对兼并那家企业感兴趣？
_____
(Neither of them)

（4）您的公司寻求与国有企业的合作还是与民营企业的合作？
_____
(I am seeking a high-tech enterprise.)

IV. 阅读、讨论和其他活动　Reading, Discussion and Other Activities

1. 根据课文对话回答问题。
Answer the following questions according to the dialogues in this lesson.

（1）张红陪史先生和白小姐去什么工厂参观？
_____

（2）这家工厂的厂长叫什么名字？他在这里工作了多少年了？
_____

（3）史先生的公司和这家工厂做过生意吗？
_____

（4）美国客人为什么要参观这家工厂？
_____

（5）厂长说引进的组装线对生产有什么帮助？
_____

（6）美国客人看到的玩具是为谁生产的？
_____

（7）美国客人觉得这家工厂怎么样？
_____

（8）你觉得今后这家中国工厂跟史先生的公司会有更多的生意吗？为什么？

_____

2. 根据阅读短文回答问题。
Answer the following questions based on the Reading Passage.

（1）中国的国有企业一般由谁投资、管理？
_____

（2）国有企业有哪些优势？
_____

（3）对那些有问题的国有企业，政府怎样进行改革？
_____

（4）在中国企业改革过程中，民营企业有什么发展？
_____

（5）在中国的外资企业主要有哪些类型？
_____

（6）无论是国有企业还是民营企业，都要怎样调整发展计划？
_____

（7）为什么现在是进入中国市场的大好机会？
_____

3. 小任务。Tasks.

A 利用图书馆或者上网，找出三家做进出口生意的中国企业。看看这些企业是国有企业还是民营企业。把你找到的信息写下来，再对其中一家企业做一个简单的介绍，在课堂上报告。你也可以参考利用本课的附录《2017年中国企业50强排行榜》。

Using the library and/or the internet, find 3 Chinese companies involved in the import or export business. Please identify these companies as state-owned or privately-run first, then write a short paragraph to give a general introduction to one of these companies and present it to your class. You may use this lesson's appendix for your reference.

B 利用图书馆或者上网，找出一条中国国有企业改革的新闻或者是民营企业承包、租赁、兼并或购买国有企业的新闻报道。把你找到的信息整理成一篇小报告。

Using the library and/or the internet, find a news report about the reform of state-owned enterprise or a news about a privately-run enterprise that has contracted, leased, merged with or purchased a state-owned enterprise in China. Please edit the information you have found into a short report in Chinese.

C 利用本课的附录《2017年中国企业50强排行榜》，找出三家国有企业和三家民营企业并简要说明它们的业务。请利用图书馆或者上网找出你所需要的信息。

Please use the Top 50 Enterprises in China (2017) in this lesson's appendix to identify 3 state-owned enterprises and 3 privately-run enterprises, then give a brief explanation about their businesses separately. Please use the library and/or the internet to find the information you need.

4. 快速复习。Quick review.

A 阅读下面的短文，复习学过的词汇和句型。
Read the following text and review vocabularies and sentence patterns that you have learned.

　　这两天史先生和白小姐的日程活动都安排得非常满。昨天他们和中方举行了初次洽谈，了解了产品的价格情况。今天他们又参观、考察了一家玩具厂。美国国际贸易公司跟这家工厂有过合作。去年他们订购的一批玩具就是在这儿生产的。产品在美国投放市场以后很受欢迎。美方对那批玩具的质量和设计都非常满意。这次史先生和白小姐来的目的一是想表示感谢，二是想亲眼看看工厂的情况。玩具厂的陈厂长接待了美国客人。他向美国客人具体介绍了工厂的设备和产品，还陪他们参观了工厂新引进的组装线和成品检验车间。工厂的管理和效率给了史先生和白小姐很深的印象。史先生告诉陈厂长他非常希望今后双方能有更多的合作。

B 问答 Q & A：

（1）这两天史先生和白小姐忙不忙？为什么？

_____

（2）美方为什么要去参观考察这家玩具厂？

_____

（3）美方对去年订购的玩具满意吗？为什么？

_____

（4）陈厂长是怎么接待美国客人的？

_____

（5）参观完了工厂以后，美国客人有什么想法（xiǎngfǎ / idea, notion, opinion）？

_____

（四）附录　Appendix

2017年中国企业50强　Top 50 Enterprises in China (2017)

2017年中国企业50强排行榜

排名	公司名称	营业收入（百万元）	利润（百万元）
1	中国石油化工股份有限公司	1930911.00	46416.00
2	中国石油天然气股份有限公司	1616903.00	7900.00
3	中国建筑股份有限公司	959765.49	29870.10
4	上海汽车集团股份有限公司	756416.17	32008.61
5	中国平安保险（集团）股份有限公司	712453.00	62394.00
6	中国移动有限公司	708421.00	108741.00
7	中国工商银行股份有限公司	675891.00	278249.00
8	中国中铁股份有限公司	643357.32	12509.16

9	中国铁建股份有限公司	629327.09	13999.61
10	中国建设银行股份有限公司	605090.00	231460.00
11	中国人寿保险股份有限公司	549771.00	19127.00
12	中国农业银行股份有限公司	506016.00	183941.00
13	中国银行股份有限公司	483630.00	164578.00
14	中国人民保险集团股份有限公司	443323.00	14245.00
15	中国交通建设股份公司	431743.43	16743.07
16	中国电信股份有限公司	352285.00	18004.00
17	中国中信股份有限公司	325907.47	28054.84
18	联想控股股份有限公司	294745.71	4851.98
19	中国联合网络通信股份有限公司	274196.78	154.07
20	中国太平洋保险集团股份有限公司	267014.00	12057.00
21	京东商城电子商务有限公司	260121.64	−3806.79
22	国药控股股份有限公司	258387.69	4647.34
23	绿地控股集团股份有限公司	247400.15	7207.30
24	万科企业股份有限公司	240477.24	21022.61
25	中国电力建设股份有限公司	238968.36	6771.81
26	中国中车股份有限公司	229722.15	11295.60
27	中国能源建设股份有限公司	222171.02	4281.29
28	中国冶金科工股份有限公司	219557.58	5375.86
29	中国恒大集团	211444.00	5091.00
30	招商银行股份有限公司	209025.00	62081.00
31	物产中大集团股份有限公司	207172.43	2154.32
32	江西铜业股份有限公司	202308.22	787.54
33	交通银行股份有限公司	193129.00	67210.00
34	中国邮政储蓄银行股份有限公司	189602.00	39801.00
35	宝山钢铁股份有限公司	185710.29	8965.51

36	中国神华能源股份有限公司	183127.00	22712.00
37	上海浦东发展银行股份有限公司	160792.00	53099.00
38	美的集团股份有限公司	159841.70	14684.36
39	兴业银行股份有限公司	157060.00	53850.00
40	中国民生银行股份有限公司	155211.00	47843.00
41	保利房地产（集团）股份有限公司	154773.28	12421.55
42	碧桂园控股有限公司	153086.98	11516.82
43	腾讯控股有限公司	151938.00	41095.00
44	苏宁云商集团股份有限公司	148585.33	704.41
45	中国海洋石油有限公司	146490.00	637.00
46	新华人寿保险股份有限公司	146173.00	4942.00
47	厦门建发股份有限公司	145590.89	2854.66
48	中国铝业股份有限公司	144065.52	402.49
49	阿里巴巴集团控股有限公司	143878.00	38393.00
50	万洲国际有限公司	143035.29	6881.42

摘自财富中文网《2017年中国企业500强排行榜（公司名单）》
http://www.fortunechina.com/fortune500/c/2017-07/31/content_287415.htm

8 价格谈判
Price Negotiations

今天，中美两家公司要就今年秋季的订单进行谈判。其中，进货的价格和数量是双方谈判的关键。今天的谈判也是史强生和白琳这次来中国的主要目的之一。

（一）对 话 Dialogue

1. 谈判成功 Successful Negotiations

史强生：王总，这两天参观了你们的工厂，也看了不少产品。现在我想听听你们的报盘。

王国安：好啊！不知道您对哪些产品感兴趣？

史强生：我想知道贵公司的毛衣和牛仔裤的价格。

李信文：毛衣的价格是每打三百六十美元，牛仔裤每打二百四十美元。

史强生：您说的价格包括运费吗？

李信文：是的，价格包括成本和运费。

白　琳：李先生，毛衣的报盘似乎比去年高了百分之十。这是为什么？

李信文：毛衣是我们的新设计。式样和质量都有很大的改进，成本也比去年高。我们不得不适当提高价格。

白　琳：即使是这样，三百六十美元一打还是贵了一些。我们是老客户了，能不能低一点儿，给百分之五的折扣？

王国安：百分之五恐怕不行。不过，如果贵公司订购一千打以上，我们可以给百分之二点五的折扣。

史强生：嗯，这个价格可以考虑。另外，我认为贵公司的牛仔裤价格也高了一点儿。目前生产牛仔裤的厂家很多，市场竞争很激烈。如果按这个价格进货，我们几乎就没有利润了。

李信文：可是我们的产品质量是国际公认的，在市场上是有竞争力的。

史强生：对！正是这个原因，我们才希望从贵公司进货。这样吧，毛衣和牛仔裤我们各订购两千打，都给百分之三的折扣，怎么样？

王国安：行！这个价格和数量都可以接受。薄利多销嘛。我们一言为定！

课文英译

2. 谈判失败 Failed Negotiations

白　琳：李先生，请问这种皮夹克的报价是多少？

李信文：皮夹克是我们今年的试销品。为了打开销路，我们准备按每打一千八百美元的特价出售。

白　琳：李先生，您大概不太清楚国际市场目前的行情。您的这个价格跟一些世界名牌产品的价格几乎差不多了！

李信文：白小姐，我相信我们产品的设计和质量不比某些世界名牌

价格谈判
Price Negotiations
8

产品差。上个月我们和一家日本公司就是按这个价格签订了合同。不过，在没有建立知名度以前，我们愿意适当降低我们的报价。请问，您的还盘是多少呢？

白　琳：如果每打在一千二百美元，我们可以考虑订购一千打。

李信文：一千二百美元一打我们太吃亏了！我们最多降价两百块，一千六百美元一打，怎么样？

白　琳：还是太贵了！如果销路不好，我们就要赔本了。我说，咱们双方再各让价两百，一千四百美元一打，好不好？

李信文：对不起，一千六是我们的底价，不能再低了。

白　琳：真遗憾！看来我们只好另找货源了。

词汇（一）　Vocabulary (1)

1.	进货	jìn huò	to purchase merchandise; to replenish stocks
2.	数量	shùliàng	quantity
3.	关键	guānjiàn	key; key point; crux
4.	报盘	bào pán	offer; quoted price; to make an offer
5.	打	dá	dozen
6.	运费	yùnfèi	transport fees; freight charge
7.	改进	gǎijìn	to improve; improvement
8.	不得不	bùdébù	have no choice but to; to have to
9.	适当	shìdàng	proper(ly)
10.	折扣	zhékòu	discount
11.	恐怕	kǒngpà	I am afraid; perhaps
12.	不行	bùxíng	won't do/work; be no good
13.	以上	yǐshàng	over...; above...; more than

14.	考虑	kǎolǜ	to consider; to think over
15.	激烈	jīliè	intense; sharp; fierce
16.	几乎	jīhū	almost; nearly
17.	利润	lìrùn	profit;
18.	公认	gōngrèn	generally recognized; universally acknowledged
19.	竞争力	jìngzhēnglì	competitiveness
20.	接受	jiēshòu	to accept
21.	薄利多销	bólì-duōxiāo	small profits but high volume
22.	一言为定	yìyán-wéidìng	that's settled then
23.	失败	shībài	to fail; failure
24.	皮夹克	píjiākè	leather jacket
25.	报价	bào jià	quoted price; offer; to quote (a price)
26.	销路	xiāolù	sales; market
27.	特价	tèjià	special/bargain price
28.	出售	chūshòu	to offer for sale; to sell
29.	名牌	míngpái	famous brand
31.	差不多	chàbuduō	about the same; similar
32.	某些	mǒuxiē	certain (people/things/etc.); some
	某	mǒu	certain; some
33.	知名度	zhīmíngdù	name recognition; reputation
34.	还盘	huán pán	counter offer; to make a counter offer
34.	降价	jiàng jià	to lower prices
35.	赔本	péi běn	to sustain losses in business
36.	让价	ràng jià	to better one's price
37.	底价	dǐjià	bottom price
38.	遗憾	yíhàn	regrettable; to regret; to feel sorry
39.	货源	huòyuán	source of goods; supply of goods

价格谈判
Price Negotiations 8

句型（一）　Sentence Patterns (1)

1. 就……进行（/举行）谈判（/会谈/洽谈）
have negotiations (talk) on...

例：① 今天，中美两家公司要就今年秋季的订单进行谈判。
② 中美政府就两国关系举行了会谈。

2. 不得不　　have no choice but to; have to

例：① 我们不得不适当提高价格。
② 你们的报盘太高，我们不得不另找货源。

3. 即使……还是……　　even (if)... still...

例：① 即使是这样，三百六十美元一打还是贵了一些。
② 即使有百分之三的折扣，这个价格还是不便宜。

4. A 不比 B + Adj.
A is not more Adj. than B (namely, A and B are about same)

例：① 我们产品的设计和质量不比某些世界名牌产品差。
② 那家公司的报价不比我们的低。

（二）阅读短文　Reading Passage

讨价还价
Bargaining

做生意、谈买卖总是要讨价还价。"漫天要价"的说法固然有一点儿夸张，不过它的确说明了中国人讨价还价的本领。

一场商业谈判的成功，常常取决于细心和耐心。开始谈判以前，认真调查市场行情，细心比较各种商品的价格，做好谈判的一切准备，这些都是取得成功的基本条件。不过，外国人到中国做生意，常常会遇到一些想不到的问题。这不但是因为文化和习惯的不同，也是因为社会制度、经济制度的不同。一个善于谈判的好手非得有耐心不可。只要你愿意理解对方，耐心地和对方交流、沟通，总能找到解决问题的办法。你在中国的生意也一定会成功。

词汇（二）　Vocabulary (2)

1.	讨价还价	tǎojià-huánjià	to bargain; to haggle
2.	买卖	mǎimai	buying and selling; business
3.	漫天要价	màntiān-yàojià	to quote an exorbitant price in anticipation of haggling
4.	说法	shuōfǎ	way of saying sth.; wording
5.	固然	gùrán	no doubt; it is true; admittedly
6.	夸张	kuāzhāng	to exaggerate; exaggeration
7.	的确	díquè	indeed; really; certainly
8.	本领	běnlǐng	ability; skills; talent
9.	取决	qǔjué	be decided by; to depend on
10.	细心	xìxīn	carefulness; thoroughness; careful(ly); thorough(ly)
11.	耐心	nàixīn	patience; patient

价格谈判
Price Negotiations
8

12.	调查	diàochá	to investigate
13.	制度	zhìdù	system
14.	善于	shànyú	be good at; be adept in
15.	好手	hǎoshǒu	expert; ace; old pro
16.	非……不可	fēi……bùkě	must...
17.	理解	lǐjiě	to understand
18.	交流	jiāoliú	to exchange (ideas/information/etc.)
19.	沟通	gōutōng	to communicate

句型（二） Sentence Patterns (2)

1. **固然……不过……**　　it is true that... but...

   例：❶ 这种说法固然有一点儿夸张，不过它的确说明了中国人讨价还价的本领。
   ❷ 您的产品固然不错，不过价格贵了一些。

2. **取决于……**　　be decided by...; depend on...

   例：❶ 一场商业谈判的成功，常常取决于细心和耐心。
   ❷ 我们这次能订购多少，完全取决于市场行情。

3. **善于……**　　to be good at...

   例：❶ 一个善于谈判的好手非得有耐心不可。
   ❷ 李经理非常善于跟外国人做生意。

4. **非……不可**　　(absolutely) must...

   例：❶ 如果你想买到又便宜又好的东西，你非得多看几家商店不可。
   ❷ 明天我非要问他这个问题不可！

157

（三）练习与活动 Exercises & Activities

I. 词汇练习 Vocabulary Exercises

1. 连词比赛。 Matching games.

按照拼音找出相应的英文并将标示该英文的字母填进"？"栏，再写出汉字。

Match each *pinyin* with its English equivalent by filling in the corresponding letter into the "?" box, and then write Chinese characters into the "汉字" box.

* 第一场 Game one:

	PINYIN	汉字	?
1	shùliàng		
2	lìrùn		
3	jìngzhēnglì		
4	shībài		
5	jīliè		
6	huán pán		
7	jiēshòu		
8	yíhàn		
9	xiāolù		
10	gōngrèn		

	English equivalent
A	profit
B	intense
C	quantity
D	counter offer
E	regrettable
F	sales; market
G	failure
H	to accept
I	generally recognized
J	competitiveness

* 第二场 Game two:

	PINYIN	汉字	?
1	díquè		
2	shāngyè		
3	nàixīn		
4	diàochá		
5	lǐjiě		
6	gōutōng		
7	zhìdù		
8	tǎojià-huánjià		

	English equivalent
A	to bargain
B	patience
C	indeed
D	to understand
E	system
F	commerce
G	to communicate
H	to investigate

8 价格谈判 / Price Negotiations

2. 字谜。Crossword puzzle.

请根据下面的提示，猜一猜是哪个生词，把它的拼音填进下面的空格里，在旁边写出汉字，最后找出谜底。

Read each clue first, and then fill in the boxes with *pinyin* of the word you guessed. You may write the characters next to each clue. Once you fill out all the boxes, find out what "the wonder word" is.

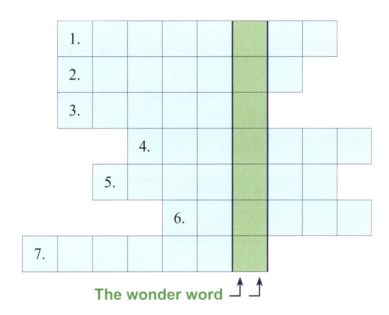

*提示 (Clues)： 　　　　　　　　　　　　　　　汉字

（1）把商品卖出去　　　　　　→

（2）东西快卖完了，需要更多的货　　→

（3）最低的价格，不能再让价了　　→

（4）运货需要花的钱　　　　　　→

（5）跟报价一样的意思　　　　　→

（6）需要再想一想　　　　　　　→

（7）做生意花的钱比赚的钱多　　→

159

3. 写出跟"价格"有关的词汇。你可以参考本课和第六课的生词表。
Write down any words and expressions in this lesson's vocabulary list associated with "price". You may also refer to the vocabulary list in Lesson 6.

（1）_____　　（2）_____　　（3）_____

（4）_____　　（5）_____　　（6）_____

（7）_____　　（8）_____　　（9）_____

（10）_____　　（11）_____　　（12）_____

4. 用下列词汇填空。每个词只能用一次。
Fill in the blanks by using the words given below. Each word can be used only once.

> 零售价　让价　底价　漫天要价　讨价还价　利润　赔本　报价
> 报盘　还盘　降低　特价　折扣　货源　行情　竞争力　降价

（1）这些名牌今天都是_____，我们快去买吧。

（2）有人很会_____,使商人不得不给他打_____。

（3）王经理，我们的_____已经是我们的_____了。如果再_____的话，我们就要_____了！请您原谅。

（4）按国际市场这种产品的_____，贵公司的_____完全没有_____。

（5）您是我们的老客户了，我方愿意适当_____价格。请问您的_____是多少呢？

（6）如果您这样_____的话，我们只好另找_____了。

（7）_____这么低，_____已经很少了。我们不能再_____了。

价格谈判
Price Negotiations 8

5. 用"以上"（或"以下" yǐxià / below, under）翻译出下面的信息。
Translate the information below by using the word "以上" (or "以下").

A
NOVA FASHION
New Beach Towel
New Price for Ordering
Over 1000 dozens: $50/dozen
Over 500 but fewer than 1000 dozens: $55/dozen
Under 500 dozens: $60/dozen

B
PARK ADMISSION RATES
Senior （age 65 and over）: $8
Adults （age 18 and over）: $10
Children & Youth （age 3 to 17）: $6
Infants （under age 3）: free

II. 句型练习（一） Sentence Pattern Exercises (1)

1. 用"就……进行（/举行）谈判（/会谈/洽谈）"和学过的词汇回答问题。例如：新订单、价格、报盘、还盘、交货时间、代理合同、贸易问题、质量问题、投资问题、引进高新技术等等。

Answer the following questions by using the pattern of "就……进行（/举行）谈判（/会谈、洽谈）" and words learned from this lesson and previous lessons. For instance, 新订单、价格、报盘、还盘、交货时间、代理合同、贸易问题、质量问题、投资问题、引进高新技术, etc.

（1）请问，这次美国贸易代表团来中国的目的是什么？

_____

（2）经理，请问明天我们要跟客户谈什么？

_____

161

（3）按照日程安排，后天双方代表要做什么？
_____

（4）按照日程安排，下个星期双方代表要做什么？
_____

2. 🎧 008 用"不得不"回答下面的问题。
Answer the following questions by using the pattern of "不得不".

（1）请问，贵厂为什么要调整今年的生产计划？
_____

（2）请问，贵公司的这种产品的报价为什么比上个月高了百分之十五？
_____

（3）贵公司是我们的老客户了，可是为什么这次决定跟日本公司签订合同？
_____

（4）做生意要有利润，可是为什么很多商店愿意给老顾客折扣呢？
_____

3. 🎧 009 "即使……还是……"和第三课里的"即使……也……"都是很常用的句型。它们的意思和用法基本一样。请用本课"即使……还是……"回答下面的问题。
Both "即使……还是……" and "即使……也……" (*seen in Lesson 3) are very common sentence patterns in Chinese. Their meanings and usages are similar. Please answer the following questions by using the pattern of "即使……还是……".

（1）如果我方同意让价百分之五，贵公司能增加进货数量吗？
_____

（2）如果我方多订购三千打，贵公司愿意给百分之十的折扣吗？
_____

（3）我们的产品是世界公认的名牌，您再考虑考虑吧？
_____

（4）让价这么多，您恐怕没有利润了吧？

_____

4. 用"A 不比 B + Adj."翻译下面的句子。
Translate the following sentences by using the pattern of "A 不比 B + Adj.":

（1）I always like to stay in this hotel when I travel to Beijing. Other 5-star hotels are more expensive than this hotel, but their services are not better than this one.

_____

（2）Please reconsider our offer. The quality of their products is not better than ours, but their price is much higher than our offer.

_____

（3）My Chinese is not very good. But it is not worse than my boss's Chinese.

_____

（4）Now it's very convenient to take a train when you travel in China. Taking a train is often not slower than taking an airplane.

_____

III. 句型练习（二） Sentence Pattern Exercises (2)

1. 用"固然……不过……"回答下面的问题。
Answer the following questions by using the pattern of "固然……不过……".

（1）这种产品的式样和质量都有了改进，您愿意进货吗？

_____

（2）我们的产品是世界名牌，贵公司为什么还要另找货源呢？

_____

（3）听说李先生非常善于讨价还价，可是为什么没有谈成那笔生意呢？
_____

（4）那家商店打那么多折扣，不怕赔本吗？（hint: 薄利多销）
_____

2. 用"取决于……"回答下面的问题。
Answer the following questions by using the pattern of "取决于……".

（1）什么是商业谈判成功的关键？
_____

（2）请问，刚投放市场的新产品怎样才能打开销路？
_____

（3）你认为怎样才能建立产品的知名度？
_____

（4）你认为外国企业怎样才能在中国取得成功？
_____

3. 用"善于……"回答下面的问题。
Answer the following questions by using the pattern of "善于".

（1）在生意上，什么样的助手是好助手？
_____

（2）为什么公司这次让李先生去美国洽谈业务？
_____

（3）为什么那种新产品能够在中国市场打开销路？
_____

（4）你最善于做什么？
_____

8 价格谈判 Price Negotiations

4. 🎧 013 用"非……不可"回答下面的问题。
Answer the following questions by using the pattern of "非……不可".

（1）为什么某些名牌商品有时候也会大打折扣？
_____

（2）要想让对方多订购一些我们的产品，我们应该怎么办？
_____

（3）今天李先生为什么好像特别忙？
_____

（4）在中国做生意怎样才能成功？
_____

IV. 阅读、讨论和其他活动　Reading, Discussion and Other Activities

1. 🎧 014 根据课文对话回答问题。
Answer the following questions according to the dialogues in this lesson.

（1）这次双方代表谈判的关键是什么？
_____

（2）美方对哪些产品感兴趣？
_____

（3）牛仔裤的报盘是多少？这个价格包括运费吗？
_____

（4）为什么今年中方提高了毛衣的价格？
_____

（5）美方觉得毛衣和牛仔裤的报价怎么样？
_____

（6）皮夹克的报价是多少？
_____

（7）中方为什么愿意适当降低皮夹克的报价？
　　_____

（8）对皮夹克的价格，美方的第一次还盘是多少？第二次还盘是多少？
　　_____

（9）中方皮夹克的底价是多少？
　　_____

（10）美方最后决定买什么？买多少？有折扣没有？
　　_____

（11）美方最后决定不买什么？为什么？
　　_____

2. 本课"阅读短文"中说："一场商业谈判的成功，常常取决于细心和耐心。"请问，在这篇"阅读短文"中，"细心"包括哪些事？"耐心"又是什么？
The Reading Passage of this lesson said, "The success of business negotiations often rests on thoroughness and patience." According to the passage, what should one do to be a careful negotiator, and what should one do to be a patient negotiator?

细心：

耐心：

3. 思考与讨论。Points for Discussion.

　　根据本课的内容和你自己的经验，谈一谈怎样才能取得商业谈判的成功，并请跟你的同学交流你的看法。

　　Based on what you learned in this lesson and your own knowledge, talk about what it takes to make a successful business deal. Please share your opinions with your classmates.

4. 角色扮演。Role-playing.

　　你和你的谈判对手已经见了几次面了。现在是双方谈判价格的时候了。请为你们的价格谈判写一个小对话并表演。请先复习本课的对话，注意谈判双方在表达询问、试探（shìtàn / to sound out）、质疑（zhìyí / to question）、解释（jiěshì / to make explanations)、建议、折中（zhézhōng / to compromise）、让步（ràngbù / to yield, to give in）、拒绝（jùjué / to decline）或遗憾时的方式，体会双方说话的语气和态度。这对你写对话会有帮助。

You and your business opponent have met several times. Now it's time to negotiate prices. Write a dialogue for such a situation and act it out with your classmates. Please review the dialogues in this lesson, paying attention to how these negotiators make inquiries, sound out and question, make explanations and suggestions, compromise or yield, or decline or express regret. When you review the dialogues, try to get a feeling about the manner of speaking (i.e. "tone" and "attitude") from both sides of negotiators. This will help you to create a "professional negotiation".

5. 快速复习。Quick review.

A 阅读下面的短文，复习学过的词汇和句型。
Read the following text and review vocabularies and sentence patterns that you have learned.

在过去的两天里，东方公司公关部主任张红陪史先生和他的助理白琳小姐参观、考察了服装厂和玩具厂。美国客人亲眼看到了这两家工厂的生产和管理情况。他们都非常满意。中美双方也初步洽谈了新的订单。今天，双方谈判的关键是进货的数量和价格问题。美方代表对目录上列出的很多产品都很感兴趣。他们具体询问了几款毛衣、牛仔裤和皮夹克的价格。美方想知道为什么毛衣和牛仔裤的报价比去年高了百分之十。中方代表告诉他们，这是因为两个原因。一是产品的质量和式样比去年更好，二是生产成本比去年高，所以价格比去年高了一些。中方表示，如果美方能增加订购数量，毛衣和牛仔裤各进货一千打以上，他们愿意让价百分之三。不过，这是中方的底价了。美方经过认真考虑，接受了这个价格，订购了两千打新款毛衣和两千打牛仔裤。遗憾的是，皮夹克的谈判没有成功。美方认为，中方的皮夹克还是试销品，还没有知名度，所以不应该这么贵。可是中方觉得美方的还盘太低。如果接受这样的价格，他们就要赔本了。中美双方都知道，现在市场竞争非常激烈，只有设计好、式样新、质量高、价格合理的产品，才能有销路。

B 问答 Q & A：

（1）美国客人参观、考察了什么地方？谁陪他们去的？

（2）在参观、考察中，他们对什么非常满意？

（3）美方具体询问了哪些产品的价格？

（4）什么原因使毛衣和牛仔裤的报价比去年高？

（5）中方同意让价百分之三的条件是什么？美方接受了没有？

（6）为什么美方认为皮夹克不应该这么贵？

（7）在牛仔裤价格的谈判中，中方为什么不愿意再让价了？

（8）因为现在市场竞争激烈，所以只有什么样的产品才能有销路？

（四）附录 Appendix

1. 报盘信实例 Sample of Offer Letter

彩虹电子公司彩色电视机产品报盘

××××公司：

　　7月20日来函收悉。感谢贵公司对我电视机产品的良好评价。现按贵方要求报盘如下：

品牌	型号	价格（美元）/台
彩虹	19寸彩色	120.00
彩虹	25寸彩色	170.00
彩虹	32寸彩色	200.00
彩虹	32寸彩色立体声	250.00

付款方式：即期信用证，美元支付。证到后七天内装运。

望以上报盘能为贵方接受，并盼早日收到贵公司的订单。

彩虹电子公司

7月30日

2. 微信截图 A Screenshot from WeChat

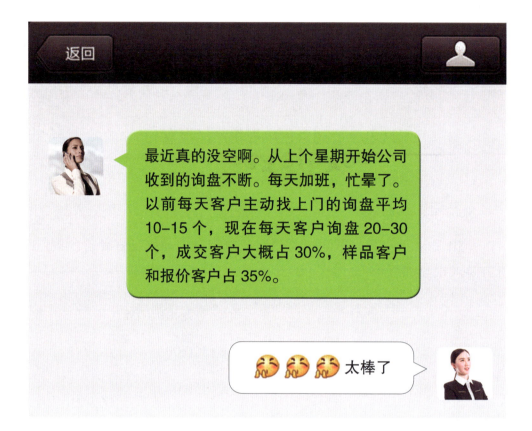

总附录
General Appendix

课文英译（第 1–8 课）
English Translation of the Text (Lesson 1–8)

Arrival in China

Mr. Johnson Smith and Miss Lynn Petty are representatives of the American International Trading Company. This time they have come to China on business. Mr. Smith previously worked in Taiwan for two years. Last year Miss Petty came to Beijing and became acquainted with Mr. Li of the Eastern Import & Export Corporation. Mr. Smith and Miss Petty both speak Chinese very well.

Dialogue

1. Entry

(At customs)

Customs Officer:	Hello! Are you here to travel?
Johnson Smith:	No, I'm here on business. Here's my passport and arrival card.
Customs Officer:	Are these two items of luggage both yours? Please open this suitcase.
Johnson Smith:	Okay, no problem.
Customs Officer:	What are these?
Johnson Smith:	These are (printed) product advertisements and merchandise samples. This one is a gift. Are these things subject to duty?
Customs Officer:	The advertisement and merchandise samples without commercial value are duty-free. Gifts above 2000 *yuan* are dutiable, so yours are fine. But you still have to fill out a customs declaration form.
Lynn Petty:	Here are our customs declaration forms, my passport and arrival card.
Customs Officer:	What is that?
Lynn Petty:	That's my good friend!
Customs Officer:	Good friend?
Lynn Petty:	(smiling) That's right... that's my computer. We're together everyday, and we're the best of friends!
Customs Officer:	(smiling) Your Chinese is really good!
Lynn Petty:	[modestly declining compliment] You're too kind!

2. Meeting Each Other

(At airport exit)

Lynn Petty:	Look, there's Mr. Li! (Waving her hands) Mr. Li, it's been a long time. Hello!
Li Xinwen:	Hello! We meet again, Miss Petty! Welcome!
Lynn Petty:	I'll make the introductions. This is the vice president of the Eastern Corporation, Mr. Li. This is my boss, Mr. Smith.
Johnson Smith:	How do you do! I'm Johnson Smith. My Chinese name is Shi Qiangsheng.
Li Xinwen:	How do you do! My name is Li Xinwen. Welcome to China!
Johnson Smith:	Thank you! Lynn has often mentioned you to me, and this time we finally meet!
Lynn Petty:	This is great! After over ten hours on an airplane, we've finally arrived in Beijing! Mr. Li, thank you for coming to the airport to meet us.
Li Xinwen:	Not at all... we're old friends. Are you finished with all the entry formalities?
Lynn Petty:	Yes. Everything went smoothly!
Li Xinwen:	Good. Let's go then. The car is right outside. Let me take you to the hotel first. (I guess) You must be tired.

Reading Passage

When in China, Speak Chinese

There are a lot of advantages to speak Chinese when you are in China. The simplest "ni hao" often makes matters easier. "Ni hao" [can] make a stern official smile at you; it [can also] lighten up serious negotiations. Don't worry that your Chinese is not very good. You will find that when you speak Chinese, Chinese people will always be very pleased, and more than willing to help you.

It's easy to make friends when you speak Chinese; and once you have good friends, you will enjoy a lot of conveniences when doing business and taking care of [various other] matters. As long as you speak Chinese every day... [just] saying as much as you can... your Chinese will get better and better.

Lesson 2

At the Hotel

Li Xinwen reserved rooms for Johnson Smith and Lynn Petty at the Great Wall Hotel. This is a 5-star hotel. Not only does it have good service and well-provided amenities, but the location is very convenient. Lynn Petty likes this place very much, but she has a lot of questions.

Dialogue

1. Checking In

Front Desk Clerk: Hello!

Li Xinwen: Hello! Yesterday I made a reservation for these two American guests. My last name is Li. Would you please look it up?

Front Desk Clerk: Are you Mr. Li of the Eastern Corporation?

Li Xinwen: Yes, my name is Li Xinwen.

Front Desk Clerk: Please have your two guests fill out the hotel guest registration form.

Li Xinwen: I reserved one standard room and one suite for you. The standard room is 650 *yuan* per day; the suite is 900 *yuan*.

Lynn Petty: Wow. That's a lot more expensive than last year! Excuse me, can I fill out the form in English?

Front Desk Clerk: That's fine. [I'm] sorry, I need to take a look at your passports.

Li Xinwen: Guests have to put down a room deposit first, right?

Front Desk Clerk: Yes, [they] may pay cash or use a credit card.

Johnson Smith: I think I'll use a credit card.

Front Desk Clerk: Very well. Your rooms are on the nineteenth floor. Here are the room cards. The elevator is over there. Thank you!

Lynn Petty: The nineteenth floor! Wonderful! The view must be great that high up!

2. Hotel Services

Lynn Petty: Hello! Could you please tell me where the laundry room is?

Hotel Maid: The self-serving laundromat is on the second floor. However, if you need laundry service, you can put the dirty clothes in a laundry bag and give them to me, or just

	leave the laundry bag in the room, and I'll come to pick it up in a little while.
Lynn Petty:	Thank you. May I ask if you have a wake-up call service?
Hotel Maid:	Yes, we do. You can dial 1-2-3-7 and tell the front desk what time you need to get up.
Lynn Petty:	Do you know where I can use the internet? I have to check my emails.
Hotel Maid:	You can access the internet at the business center on the second floor. If you bring a [laptop] computer with you, you can use the internet in your room for free. No password is needed.
Lynn Petty:	That's fantastic! Does the hotel have a gym and swimming pool?
Hotel Maid:	Of course! [Please] take the elevator to the top floor. The gym and swimming pool are right there.
Lynn Petty:	(feels a bit embarrassed) One more thing—do you know where I can change [dollars into] RMB?
Hotel Maid:	Foreign currency exchange is done right at the service desk in the lobby.
Johnson Smith:	(smile) I am sorry, could you please tell me what floor the restaurant is on? After asking so many questions, this young lady must be hungry!

Reading Passage

Chinese Hotels

In China, hotels [can] also be called *jiǔdiàn*, *fàndiàn* or *bīnguǎn*. The best hotels are five-star hotels, and naturally they are also the most expensive. The Hilton Beijing Wangfujing Hotel (*jiǔdiàn*) in Beijing, the Jinjiang Hotel (*fàndiàn*) in Shanghai, and the Baiyun Hotel (*bīnguǎn*) in Guangzhou, etc., are all great hotels of this kind. Generally speaking, hotels with three-star and higher rankings provide complete amenities, normally including restaurants, gift shop, gym, beauty salon, laundry room, business center, and so on. These amenities are very convenient, especially the business center. At a business center, you can access the internet, send emails, and use a computer, printer, or copy machine. Many hotels also provide services like foreign currency exchange, ticket booking, car rental and local sight-seeing tours, etc. If you intend to stay in a hotel in China, it would be best to have a travel agency make reservations for you, or go online to make a reservation. You can ask a friend (in China) to help, or you can call the hotel yourself.

Lesson 3

Formal Meeting

Today was the first formal meeting between the Chinese and American representatives. President Wang Guo'an welcomed the Americans on behalf of the Eastern Import & Export Corporation. Mr. Johnson Smith explained the objectives of this visit to the Chinese party on behalf of the American International Trading Company.

Dialogue

1. Greetings and Introductions

Wang Guo'an:	Welcome, welcome! We're honored to have you here.
Li Xinwen:	Let me make introductions. This is the CEO of Asia Region for the American International Trading Company, Mr. Johnson Smith. This is his assistant, Miss Lynn Petty. This is the president of our company, Mr. Wang Guo'an. This is the director of the Department of Public Relations, Ms. Zhang Hong.
Johnson Smith:	It's a pleasure to meet you! Hello! (shaking hands) Here's my business card. Please kindly give me your advice.
Wang Guo'an:	You flatter us. Here's my business card. We hope you will offer us advice in the future, too.
Johnson Smith:	You're too kind!
Wang Guo'an:	Let's sit down and talk. (pouring tea) Please have some tea. Did you rest well last night?
Johnson Smith:	I had a very nice rest. The hotel is comfortable, and the service is very attentive. Thank you for the arrangements.
Wang Guo'an:	Don't mention it—it's [only] what we should do. If you have any problems while you're in Beijing, please contact me [or] Mr. Li anytime or let Director Zhang Hong know.
Zhang Hong:	Here's my business card with my office phone number and cellphone numbers.
Johnson Smith, Lynn Petty:	Thank you! Thank you!
Li Xinwen:	President Wang, Miss Lynn Petty is our old friend. She stayed at the Great Wall Hotel when she came to Beijing last summer, too.
Wang Guo'an:	That's great! Welcome to China once again, Miss Petty!
Lynn Petty:	Thank you! Mr. Li was a great help to me last time, and it was a pleasure working together. I just love Beijing.

2. Explaining the Objectives of the Visit

Johnson Smith:	Our purpose in making this trip to China is to confer with you about the new order for this autumn and the conclusion of the agency contract. In addition, if it's possible, we would like to visit a few factories to take a look at production conditions.
Wang Guo'an:	Okay. We'd like to schedule the first talk for tomorrow morning. As for the matter of visiting factories, Mr. Li is getting in touch with the men who are in charge there. We'll have him fill you in a moment.
Lynn Petty:	If there is time, we also hope to be able to visit Shanghai and Shenzhen for an on-the-spot investigation of the investment environment.
Li Xinwen:	I don't think there will be a problem with any of these [requests]. We can discuss the itinerary arrangements this afternoon.
Johnson Smith:	That's good. We really like to settle the itinerary as early as possible.
Zhang Hong:	President Wang is planning to invite everyone to dinner tonight to welcome Mr. Smith and Miss Petty. Miss Petty, I'll pick you up at the hotel at 6:30, okay?
Lynn Petty:	Okay! We'll be waiting for you in the lobby at 6:30.

Reading Passage

Etiquette of Meeting for Guests and Hosts

It is customary for Chinese people to shake hands to express welcome, gratitude or friendliness. When a guest and a host meet, the host should first shake the guest's hand as a gesture of greeting. Chinese are not accustomed to hugging. It's even uncomfortable for old friends to hug when they meet.

Saying certain words to express greetings is definitely a part of etiquette of meeting for guests and hosts. For instance, "*nǐ hǎo* (how are you)" "*nín zuìjìn zěnmeyàng* (how are you doing recently)" "*hěn gāoxìng jiàn dào nǐ* (very happy to meet you)" "*xìnghuì* (to be honored to meet)" "*jiǔyǎng* (I have heard of your name for a long time)" and "*qǐng duō zhǐjiào* (please give me your advice)". These greeting words and courteous phrases are often used.

Many Chinese like to exchange business cards when they first meet someone. When somebody gives you a business card, you should accept it with both hands as an expression of courtesy. Business cards can help you remember his (or her) name, and they also make it easy to get in touch in the future. Incidentally, some people like to list a lot of official titles on their business cards. Don't worry—it's enough to remember the first title. Generally speaking, the title listed first is the most important one.

Lesson 4

Itinerary Arrangements

Johnson Smith and Lynn Petty plan to stay in China for about a week. Besides talking over business matters with their Chinese [associates] and visit [a few] factories in Beijing, they also plan to visit Shanghai for seeing a commodity trade fair and visit Shenzhen for an on-the-spot investigation at an industrial park as well as a start-up company. Now Mr. Li Xinwen is going to discuss the itinerary arrangements with them.

Dialogue

1. Discussing Itinerary Arrangements

Li Xinwen: Mr. Smith, Miss Petty, shall we talk over the itinerary arrangements now?

Johnson Smith: Sure. We have a lot of matters to take care of during this trip to China, and there are quite a few places that we want to visit, so we must plan [our schedule] carefully. Mr. Li, we intend to stay in China for a total of eight days. Do you think that will be enough time?

Li Xinwen: It sounds like that the time is a bit tight. However, if we make a reasonable arrangement, there shouldn't be a problem.

Lynn Petty: Mr. Li is very experienced in planning itineraries. When I was in Beijing last year, he scheduled each day full [of activities]. We discussed business in the morning, toured in the afternoon, and watched performances at night. There wasn't even time to call my boyfriend! (laughing)

Li Xinwen: (laughing) I'm sorry, Miss Petty. This time we'll make sure to set aside a time just for you to make phone calls.

Lynn Petty: That won't be necessary! We've already broken up anyway!

2. Revising Itinerary Arrangements

Li Xinwen: This is how I'm thinking of arranging the itinerary: [You'll spend] the first five days in Beijing and the last three days in Shanghai and Shenzhen—two days in Shanghai and one day in Shenzhen. What do you think?

Johnson Smith: Isn't just one day too little time to stay in Shenzhen? I've heard that the investment environment in Shenzhen is excellent. The development of economy is very fast,

	especially the development of new high-tech industry. I'd really like to have the chance to take a look for myself!
Li Xinwen:	In that case, we can change the schedule to four days in Beijing and two days each in Shanghai and Shenzhen. Will that work?
Lynn Petty:	I think that will suit us better. Mr. Li, may I ask what activities you have planned for us in Beijing?
Li Xinwen:	In Beijing, besides discussing business, we will visit an apparel factory and a toy factory, [as well as] tour the Imperial Palace and the Great Wall.
Johnson Smith:	That's a good and thoughtful schedule. Mr. Li, we've put you into too much trouble!
Li Xinwen:	It's nothing more than what I should do. Also, tonight at 7:00 we have the welcome banquet, and tomorrow night Factory Director Qian of the apparel factory would like to take both of you out to eat. The night after that I would like to treat you to Beijing roast duck...
Johnson Smith:	Mr. Li, you're too gracious!
Lynn Petty:	(to Johnson Smith) I guess now you know why I gained ten pounds last year? (laughing)

Reading Passage

Eat Well, Have Fun and Do Well in Business

China is a vast land with a large population and a very busy transportation system. Foreigners traveling in China not only have problems with the language; they also commonly run into unforeseen hassles. If you intend to go on a business trip to China, you should definitely have your travel plans worked out [first]. You may want to inform your host organization in China about what places you would like to tour, visit and do on-the-spot investigation, and ask them to arrange the itinerary for you as well as booking hotel, airplane ticket or train ticket. You may also send your itinerary to your Chinese associates in advance by email. It will make it easier for them to prepare for your visit.

Whether you are going to China on business or on a personal visit, sight-seeing and banquets are both indispensable parts of Chinese itinerary arrangements. In particular, invitations to meals can be so frequent as to even become a burden. Chinese think that treating people to meals is conducive to establishing relationships and developing friendships. After eating a sumptuous dinner, who can still say "no" to the host?

Lesson 5

Attending a Banquet

President Wang Guo'an held a banquet to welcome Mr. Johnson Smith and Miss Lynn Petty on behalf of the Eastern Import & Export Corporation. Director Ma of the Foreign Trade Bureau also attended. Johnson Smith and Lynn Petty both thought the banquet was very sumptuous.

Dialogue

1. Please Take the Seats of Honor

(At the restaurant)

Wang Guo'an: Mr. Smith, Miss Petty, you've arrived! Please come in!

Johnson Smith: Thank you!

Lynn Petty: This restaurant is beautifully decorated!

Zhang Hong: Yes, this is one of Beijing's most famous restaurants. Everyone likes to come here.

Wang Guo'an: Here, I'll introduce you. This is Director Ma of the Foreign Trade Bureau. This is Mr. Smith and Miss Petty of the American International Trading Company.

Director Ma: Welcome! Welcome to China! (shaking hands) This last couple of days must have been tiring!

Johnson Smith: Not too bad, really. We had a little jet lag, but we rested well yesterday. President Wang has taken care of everything for us.

Wang Guo'an: Everybody please take your seats! Mr. Smith, Miss Petty, you are our guests. Please be seated here at the seats of honor. Director Ma, please sit here also!

Director Ma: You are the host, [so] it's only right for you to sit with the guests!

Wang Guo'an: No, you are a [government] leader and should sit with our honored guests. I'll sit next to you. Come, everyone, please just take a seat anywhere you like!

2. Cheers!

Wang Guo'an: We've gathered here tonight to welcome Mr. Smith and Miss Petty. Why don't we all have a little something to drink first? Mr. Smith, would you like Maotai or red wine?

Johnson Smith: I've heard that Maotai liquor is legendary. I'll have the Maotai.

Wang Guo'an: And you, Miss Petty?

Lynn Petty:	I'm really not much of a drinker. I'll have the wine, I guess.
Wang Guo'an:	Confucius said, "Isn't it a joy to have friends coming from distant places?" Now, let's drink a toast to welcome Mr. Smith and Miss Petty! (everyone toasts)
Director Ma:	Mr. Smith, please have something to eat. These are all hors d'oeuvres. In a little while [they'll bring out] the main dishes and the soup. Here, taste this! (Director Ma uses serving-chopsticks to place some food on Mr. Smith's plate)
Johnson Smith:	Thank you! I'll help myself.

(The waiters serve the food)

Zhang Hong:	The dishes we're having today are all specialties of this restaurant. Miss Petty, try this. Do you like it?
Lynn Petty:	Mmm...it's delicious!
Zhang Hong:	Since it's good, eat some more! Now taste this.
Lynn Petty:	(laughing) Thank you. There are so many dishes on the table that I couldn't even try them all!
Johnson Smith:	Mr. Wang, I'd like to propose a toast to you in appreciation of the warm reception you all have given us!
Wang Guo'an:	Okay. Let's drink together in anticipation of our satisfactory and successful cooperation!

Chinese Banquets

Chinese food is famous throughout the world, and eating is naturally an extremely important matter in China. Chinese banquets are always very sumptuous. It's said that the celebrated "complete Manchu and Chinese banquet" had over 100 courses. Even ordinary banquets have over ten courses. During a banquet, distinguished guests and the host are placed at the seats of honor. Generally speaking, the seats facing the door or entrance are the seats of honor. Of course no banquet is complete without liquor. The meaning of "*ganbei*" is to finish drinking everything in your glass. If you don't want to become drunk immediately, however, you had better not finish your drink at one go. Chinese are accustomed to drinking and eating [various] dishes first and then eating rice and soup. So, the sequence of courses is: first, hors d'oeuvres (or so-called "cold dish"); then, stir-fried dishes and the main dishes; and lastly, rice, soup and dessert. The old generation of Chinese people has another custom, which is that the host should serve the guest food (namely: to pick up food with chopsticks and place them in the guest's bowl or plate). This expresses both sincerity and hospitality on the part of the host. If you are not used to this [custom], you can say to the host, "Thank you. I'll help myself."

Lesson 6

Preliminary Negotiations

Today the representatives of the Chinese and American companies are going to conduct preliminary negotiations. The Eastern Corporation's [representatives] have made extensive preparations for these negotiations. First, they have invited the American representatives watched an introductory video of products. Then they've showed [their guests] product samples. Johnson Smith and Lynn Petty are particularly interested in some of the new designs.

Dialogue

1. Introducing Products

(In the conference room)

Wang Guo'an: Mr. Smith, Miss Petty, we have just watched a product video. Next, we will have Manager Li acquaint the two of you about our products and prices with details. Is that all right with you?

Johnson Smith: Sure. Discussing business is precisely why we've come. I'm really eager to know what products your company is able to offer this year.

Li Xinwen: Here is our product catalogue for this year. [to both Mr. Smith and Miss Petty] Please go ahead and look through it.

Johnson Smith: Mr. Li, are these all this year's new designs?

Li Xinwen: Eighty percent are new designs; only the ones in the back are traditional products that we continue to carry. I've also brought along some samples for you to take a look at. (picking up the samples)

Lynn Petty: Oh, how pretty! Mr. Li, I just love these designs, especially this sweater. The color and style are both very nice.

Li Xinwen: (smiling) This one? This was designed according to the suggestions you made last time. Have you forgotten, Miss Petty?

Lynn Petty: (laughing) Really? If that's the case, how do you plan to thank me?

2. Inquiring Prices

Johnson Smith: President Wang, the products your company is putting out this year have a lot of appeal, especially these new designs. May I ask if the prices listed in the catalogue are retail or wholesale prices?

Wang Guo'an:	The prices in the catalogue are all retail prices. Wholesale prices are fifteen to twenty-five percent lower. In addition, some new products have special sale prices.
Lynn Petty:	Mr. Li, I noticed that there are some products with no price listed in the catalogue. Can you tell me their prices?
Li Xinwen:	The ones with no listed price are all trial items. (pointing to the catalogue) For instance, this pair of jeans and these sweaters, are both being produced by the manufacturer on a trial basis. If your company is interested, the prices can be negotiated individually using the current market prices of similar products as a reference.
Johnson Smith:	From what I understand, the price of your company's suits appears to be a little higher than that of other companies. Why is that?
Li Xinwen:	I suppose our price being slightly higher has something to do with the product's quality and design, especially this brand. It is well received among our customers. You can make further comparisons [if you like].
Johnson Smith:	Good. I would like to take these materials back with me and look through them carefully.
Wang Guo'an:	(looking at his watch) Oh, it's already after twelve o'clock. What do you say we eat lunch first and then continue our discussion?
Lynn Petty:	(jokingly) I agree... my stomach has already started negotiating with me!

Reading Passage

It Pays to Shop Around

Whether it's in shopping or in business, price is always one of the matters of most concern to both the buyer and the seller. China has an old saying that goes, "Compare the merchandise at three shops, and you won't come to grief." It [just] means that if you want to buy something, it's best to compare the prices and qualities at several different stores. This is the only way to avoid getting a bad deal; it's [also] the only way to buy quality things that are both inexpensive and satisfactory.

Ever since the implementation of the policies of reform and opening to the outside world in 1979, China's market economy has expanded greatly. Customers now have more alternatives in the price, quality and variety of merchandise. On the one hand, market competition has brought more opportunities; but on the other hand, it has also brought more challenges. If you plan to do business in China, you definitely need to understand China's market conditions in advance and fully grasp the related information. *The Art of War* says you can only be successful if you know yourself [as well as] know the opponent. This is also true in business.

Lesson 7

Visiting a Factory

After the Chinese and American [representatives] concluded their first business discussion, Zhang Hong accompanied Johnson Smith and Lynn Petty on a tour of the toy factory [where] a batch of toys from their company's last order was manufactured. They were deeply impressed by the toy factory's management and production efficiency.

Dialogue

1. In the Reception Room

Zhang Hong: Factory Director Chen, your guests have arrived!

Factory Director Chen: Welcome! Welcome to our factory! I'll introduce myself. My name is Chen Dafang, and I'm the factory director here. You must be Mr. Smith of the American International Trading Company!

Johnson Smith: That's right... I'm Johnson Smith. This is my assistant, Miss Lynn Petty.

Lynn Petty: How do you do, Factory Director Chen! Director Zhang has said that the toys that we ordered last year were manufactured right here. Is that so?

Factory Director Chen: Yes, yes. I remember there was a rush to deliver that batch of toys before Christmas. Mr. Smith, Miss Petty, was your company satisfied with the products?

Johnson Smith: Very satisfied. We've come today [for two reasons]: first, to express our gratitude to your factory; and second, to take a look at production conditions with our own eyes.

Factory Director Chen: You're too gracious, Mr. Smith! How about we first watch a video in order to know the basic information about our factory, then I will accompany everyone to see the workshops in (our) production area. What do you say, Director Zhang?

Zhang Hong: Sure! (to Johnson Smith and Lynn Petty) If you have any questions, you may ask Director Chen at any time. He has been here more than 10 years and he knows everything about this place.

Johnson Smith & Lynn Petty: Okay!

2. At the Production Area

Factory Director Chen: This is our factory's assembly workshop. After products are assembled here, they're sent to the finished products workshop to undergo a quality inspection.

Lynn Petty:	Factory Director Chen, not only is your workshop well-run, but the equipment is state-of-the-art.
Factory Director Chen:	[modestly declines compliment] You flatter me. Last year we brought in these two assembly lines from abroad. Now not only have our costs gone down, but our output is also three times higher than it was two years ago. Our quality has also improved.
Johnson Smith:	Are these cartoon figures being assembled right now going to be exported?
Factory Director Chen:	Yes. These toys are all being manufactured for Disney. They're planning to put them on the market this fall, so time is pressing.
Lynn Petty:	They're too cute! I'm sure they'll be very popular!
Johnson Smith:	Factory Director Chen, I'm very impressed by your factory. I hope we can work together even more from now on.
Factory Director Chen:	That's great! Let's keep in close contact in the future!

Reading Passage

Chinese Enterprises

Enterprises in China can be roughly divided into several categories: state-owned enterprises, privately-run enterprises, and foreign or foreign-funded enterprises. State-owned enterprises are funded and operated by the central government or local governments. Because they have government support, they enjoy a certain advantage [in access to] financial resources, raw materials, technology and marketing. However, some state-owned enterprises have been poorly managed and have been suffering financial loss over a long period of time. Privately-run enterprises in China have grown very rapidly over the last twenty to thirty years, and they now provide state-owned enterprises with some stiff competition. Presently, the Chinese government is actively pushing the reform of state-owned enterprise, and encouraging individuals or privately-owned enterprises to take over those ineffective state-owned enterprises by means of contract, lease, merger or acquisition. During this course of reforming, privately-run enterprises have gradually developed into two types: state-owned but privately-run enterprise and privately-owned and privately-run enterprise. There are two main types of foreign enterprises in China, which include wholly foreign owned enterprises and Sino-foreign joint venture enterprises. Many Fortune Global 500 companies have their investments in China.

Enterprises are greatly impacted by the economic policies of the Chinese government. Whether state-owned or privately-run, every business must accommodate its expansion plans to the government's economic policies. [At present,] spurred on by the Chinese government's policy of reform and opening-up, many state-owned and privately-run enterprises are actively seeking collaboration with foreign enterprises. This is an excellent opportunity to enter the Chinese market.

Lesson 8

Price Negotiations

Today the Chinese and American companies are going to negotiate the order for this fall. The purchasing price and quantity will be the key points in the negotiations for both parties. Today's negotiations are one of the primary reasons Johnson Smith and Lynn Petty have made this trip to China.

Dialogue

1. Successful Negotiations

Johnson Smith: President Wang, over the last couple of days we have toured your factories and looked at quite a few products. Now I'd like to hear your prices.

Wang Guo'an: Sure! Do you have any particular products in mind?

Johnson Smith: I'd like to know the price of your sweaters and jeans.

Li Xinwen: The sweaters are 360 U.S. dollars per dozen; the jeans are 240 U.S. dollars per dozen.

Johnson Smith: Do the prices you've stated include freight charges?

Li Xinwen: Yes, they include cost and freight.

Lynn Petty: Mr. Li, the quote for the sweaters appears to be 10% higher than last year. Why is this?

Li Xinwen: This sweater is our new design. The style and quality are both greatly improved, and the cost is also higher than last year. We have no choice but to raise the price accordingly.

Lynn Petty: Even so, 360 U.S. dollars per dozen is still pretty expensive. We're longtime clients... can't you go a little lower, [say], give us a 5% discount?

Wang Guo'an: I'm afraid 5% is impossible. However, if your company orders over 1000 dozen, we can give a 2.5% discount.

Johnson Smith: Hmm, we can consider this price. Also, I think your jeans are a little overpriced as well. There are a lot of manufacturers producing jeans at present, and competition is fierce. If we buy at this price, we won't make a profit!

Li Xinwen: But the quality of our products is internationally recognized, and they are competitive in the market.

Johnson Smith: Right! That's precisely why we hope to buy from your company. How about we order 2000 dozen each of the sweaters and jeans, and you give us a 3% discount on both?

Wang Guo'an: Okay! That price and quantity are acceptable to us—"small profits but high volume." It's settled then!

2. Failed Negotiations

Lynn Petty: Mr. Li, may I ask what your quote is for this type of leather jacket?

Li Xinwen: That leather jacket is [one of] our trial products for this year. In order to establish a place for it in the market, we're prepared to sell at the special price of 1800 U.S. dollars per dozen.

Lynn Petty: Mr. Li, you must not be very clear about the current situation on the international market. Your price is almost the same as the price of some world famous brands!

Li Xinwen: Miss Petty, I believe the design and quality of our product can compare favorably with certain world famous brands. Last month we signed a contract with a Japanese company at this very price. However, while our name recognition is still low, we are willing to lower our price accordingly. May I ask what your counter offer is?

Lynn Petty: If [the price is lowered to] 1200 U.S. dollars per dozen, we can consider ordering 1000 dozen.

Li Xinwen: Our losses would be too great at 1200 U.S. dollars per dozen! The most we will go down is 200 dollars. How about 1600 U.S. dollars per dozen?

Lynn Petty: That's still too expensive! If sales aren't good, we will have to sell at a loss. Why don't we both concede 200 more [and settle on] 1400 U.S. dollars per dozen?

Li Xinwen: I'm sorry. 1600 is our bottom price... we can't go any lower.

Lynn Petty: That's too bad! It looks like we have no choice but to look for another supplier.

Reading Passage

Bargaining

Bargaining is an essential part of doing business. The saying, "quote a price so vast as to cover the heavens," is a bit of an exaggeration no doubt; but it really is a good illustration of the knack Chinese have for bargaining.

The success of business negotiations often rests on thoroughness and patience. Before beginning to negotiate, [one should] diligently investigate market conditions, carefully compare the prices of various goods, and thoroughly prepare for the coming negotiations. These are all basic determinants of success. However, foreigners doing business in China often run into some unexpected problems. This is not only due to differences in culture and customs; it's also a result of differences in social and economic systems. An adept negotiator must have patience. As long as you're willing to understand the other party and patiently communicate with him or her, you will always be able to find a solution to your problems. And your business dealings in China will certainly succeed.

总词汇表（上册）
Vocabulary Index (Volume I)

A

1	按照	ànzhào	according to; on the basis of	L.6a

B

2	白琳	Bái Lín	*a name*	L.1a
3	白云宾馆	Báiyún Bīnguǎn	Baiyun Hotel	L.2b
4	百分之……	bǎifēnzhī……	... percent	L.6a
5	办事情	bàn shìqing	to attend to matters; to handle affairs	L.1b
6	办手续	bàn shǒuxù	to go through formalities/procedures	L.1a
7	帮忙	bāng máng	to help; to give a hand	L.2b
8	磅	bàng	pound	L.4a
9	包括	bāokuò	to include	L.3b
10	保留	bǎoliú	to retain; to continue to have	L.6a
11	报价	bào jià	quoted price; offer; to quote (a price)	L.8a
12	报盘	bào pán	offer; quoted price; to make an offer	L.8a
13	北京烤鸭	Běijīng Kǎoyā	Beijing roast duck	L.4a
14	本厂	běn chǎng	one's own factory; this factory	L.7a
15	本领	běnlǐng	ability; skills; talent	L.8b
16	变得	biànde	have become; to turn (into)	L.1b
17	便于	biànyú	easy to; convenient for	L.3b
18	标准	biāozhǔn	standard; typical	L.2a
19	标准间	biāozhǔnjiān	standard room	L.2a
20	宾馆	bīnguǎn	hotel; guesthouse	L.2b
21	宾主	bīnzhǔ	guest and host	L.3b
22	并	bìng	and; besides; moreover	L.7b
23	薄利多销	bólì-duōxiāo	small profits but high volume	L.8a
24	不得不	bùdébù	have no choice but to; to have to	L.8a
25	不敢当	bùgǎndāng	I don't deserve your compliment; you flatter me.	L.3a
26	不好意思	bù hǎoyìsi	to feel embarrassed; sorry	L.2a

27	不善	búshàn	not good; bad; not good at	L.7b
28	不少	bùshǎo	not few; many	L.7b
29	不行	bùxíng	won't do/work; be no good	L.8a
30	布置	bùzhì	to decorate; to arrange	L.5a

C

31	参照	cānzhào	to refer to; to consult	L.6a
32	差不多	chàbuduō	about the same; similar	L.8a
33	产量	chǎnliàng	output; yield	L.7a
34	产品	chǎnpǐn	product	L.1a
35	产业	chǎnyè	industry; estate; property	L.4a
36	尝	cháng	to taste	L.5a
37	长城	Chángchéng	the Great Wall	L.4a
38	长期	chángqī	over a long period of time; long-term	L.7b
39	厂家	chǎngjiā	manufacturer	L.6a
40	厂长	chǎngzhǎng	factory director/manager	L.4a
41	超过	chāoguò	to exceed; to surpass	L.1a
42	车间	chējiān	workshop	L.7a
43	成本	chéngběn	cost	L.7a
44	成功	chénggōng	succeed; success; successful	L.5a
45	成品	chéngpǐn	finished products	L.7a
46	成为	chéngwéi	to become; to turn into	L.4b
47	承包	chéngbāo	to contract	L.7b
48	吃亏	chī kuī	to suffer loss; to come to grief; to be at a disadvantage	L.6b
49	充分	chōngfèn	full; fully	L.6b
50	出差	chū chāi	be away on official business or on a business trip	L.4b
51	出口	chūkǒu	export; to export; exit	L.1a
52	出售	chūshòu	to offer for sale; to sell	L.8a
53	出席	chūxí	to attend; be present (at a banquet, etc.)	L.5a
54	初步	chūbù	initial; preliminary	L.6a
55	初次	chūcì	the first time	L.3b
56	传统	chuántǒng	traditional; tradition	L.6a
57	创业	chuàngyè	to start an undertaking; business start-up	L.4a

58	创业公司	chuàngyè gōngsī	start-up company	L.4a
59	吹	chuī	to blow; to play (a wind instrument); to break up (with boyfriend/girlfriend); to fall through (of plans)	L.4a
60	次序	cìxù	order; sequence	L.5b
61	促销价	cùxiāojià	sale price	L.6a
62	催	cuī	to urge; to hasten; to press	L.7a

D

63	打	dá	dozen	L.8a
64	打印机	dǎyìnjī	printer	L.2b
65	大菜	dàcài	main dish	L.5a
66	大厅	dàtīng	lobby	L.2a
67	大致	dàzhì	roughly; approximately; in general	L.7a
68	代表	dàibiǎo	representative; to represent	L.1a
69	代理	dàilǐ	agency; representation; to act as agent; agent	L.3a
70	待	dāi	to stay	L.4a
71	袋	dài	bag	L.2a
72	担心	dān xīn	to worry; to feel anxious	L.1b
73	单	dān	list; form; voucher	L.1a
74	单位	dānwèi	unit; organization; place of work	L.4b
75	当地	dāngdì	local	L.2b
76	倒	dào	to pour (tea, etc.)	L.3a
77	到达	dàodá	to arrive	L.1a
78	道	dào	a measure word for dishes; courses	L.5b
79	的确	díquè	indeed; really; certainly	L.8b
80	登记	dēng jì	registration; to register; to check in	L.1a
81	登记卡	dēngjìkǎ	registration card	L.1a
82	等等	děngděng	et cetera; and so on	L.2b
83	迪士尼	Díshìní	Disney	L.7a
84	底价	dǐjià	bottom price	L.8a
85	地点	dìdiǎn	place; site; location	L.2a
86	地区	dìqū	region; area; district	L.3a
87	电梯	diàntī	elevator	L.2a
88	调查	diàochá	to investigate	L.8b

89	顶楼	dǐnglóu	top floor; attic	L.2a
90	订单	dìngdān	order sheet; order	L.3a
91	订购	dìnggòu	to order (goods)	L.7a
92	订票	dìngpiào	to book tickets; ticket booking	L.2b
93	东方进出口公司	Dōngfāng Jìnchūkǒu Gōngsī	Eastern Import & Export Corporation	L.1a
94	逗留	dòuliú	to stay; to stop	L.4a
95	独资企业	dúzī qǐyè	single venture enterprise	L.7b
96	对方	duìfāng	the opposite side; the other party	L.3b
97	对手	duìshǒu	opponent; adversary	L.7b
98	兑换	duìhuàn	to exchange; to convert	L.2a
99	顿	dùn	a measure word for meals	L.4b

F

100	发展	fāzhǎn	development; to develop	L.4a
101	繁忙	fánmáng	(very) busy; hectic	L.4b
102	反正	fǎnzhèng	anyway; anyhow; in any case	L.4a
103	房卡	fángkǎ	key card; room card	L.2a
104	非……不可	fēi……bùkě	must...	L.8b
105	费心	fèixīn	to give a lot of care; to take a lot of trouble	L.4a
106	分为	fēnwéi	to divide (into)	L.7b
107	丰盛	fēngshèng	rich; sumptuous	L.4b
108	服务台	fúwùtái	service desk; front desk	L.2a
109	服装	fúzhuāng	dress; clothing	L.4a
110	服装厂	fúzhuāngchǎng	clothing factory	L.4a
111	付	fù	to pay	L.2a
112	负担	fùdān	burden	L.4b
113	赴宴	fù yàn	to attend a banquet	L.4b
114	复印机	fùyìnjī	copy machine; duplicator	L.2b
115	副	fù	vice; associate	L.1a
116	副总经理	fù zǒngjīnglǐ	vice president; vice general manager	L.1a

G

117	改革	gǎigé	reform; to reform	L.6b
118	改革开放政策	Gǎigé Kāifàng Zhèngcè	the Reform and Opening-up to the Outside World policy (*first implemented in 1979)	L.6b

119	改进	gǎijìn	to improve; improvement	L.8a
120	赶	gǎn	to rush; to hurry; to make a dash for	L.7a
121	干杯	gān bēi	to drink a toast; Cheers!; Bottoms up!	L.5a
122	高新科技	gāo-xīn kējì	advanced and new technology	L.4a
123	个人	gèrén	individual; oneself	L.7b
124	工厂	gōngchǎng	factory	L.4a
125	工业园区	gōngyè yuánqū	industrial park	L.4a
126	公共关系部	Gōnggòng Guānxì Bù	Department of Public Relations	L.3a
127	公筷	gōngkuài	serving-chopsticks; chopsticks for serving food	L.5a
128	公认	gōngrèn	generally recognized; universally acknowledged	L.8a
129	公司	gōngsī	company	L.1a
130	沟通	gōutōng	to communicate	L.8b
131	购买	gòumǎi	to purchase; to buy	L.7b
132	鼓励	gǔlì	to encourage; to urge	L.7b
133	固然	gùrán	no doubt; it is true; admittedly	L.8b
134	故宫	Gùgōng	the Imperial Palace	L.4a
135	顾客	gùkè	customer	L.6b
136	关键	guānjiàn	key; key point; crux	L.8a
137	官员	guānyuán	officer; official	L.1a
138	管理	guǎnlǐ	to manage; to run; to administer; management	L.7a
139	光临	guānglín	presence (of a guest, etc.); to be present	L.3a
140	广告	guǎnggào	advertisement; commercial	L.1a
141	广州	Guǎngzhōu	*a city name*	L.2b
142	贵宾	guìbīn	honored/distinguished guest	L.5a
143	国际	guójì	international	L.1a
144	国外	guówài	overseas; abroad	L.7a
145	国有	guóyǒu	state-owned	L.7b
146	过程	guòchéng	course (of events); process	L.7b
147	过目	guò mù	to look over (a paper/list/etc.; so as to check or approve; to go over	L.6a

H

148	海关	hǎiguān	customs	L.1a
149	行情	hángqíng	business conditions; market conditions; uotation	L.6b

150	好好儿	hǎohāor	carefully; to the best of one's ability	L.4a
151	好客	hàokè	hospitable	L.5b
152	好手	hǎoshǒu	expert; ace; old pro	L.8b
153	合理	hélǐ	reasonable; rational	L.4a
154	合同	hétóng	contract; agreement	L.3a
155	合资企业	hézī qǐyè	joint venture enterprise	L.7b
156	合作	hézuò	to cooperate; to work together; cooperation	L.3a
157	后天	hòutiān	day after tomorrow	L.4a
158	互联网	hùliánwǎng	internet	L.2a
159	护照	hùzhào	passport	L.1a
160	还盘	huán pán	counter offer; to make a counter offer	L.8a
161	环境	huánjìng	environment	L.3a
162	会客室	huìkèshì	reception room	L.7a
163	会谈	huìtán	talks; to talk	L.3a
164	货	huò	goods; commodities	L.6b
165	货样	huòyàng	merchandise/product sample	L.1a
166	货源	huòyuán	source of goods; supply of goods	L.8a

J

167	积极	jījí	positive(ly); active(ly)	L.7b
168	激烈	jīliè	intense; sharp; fierce	L.8a
169	级	jí	rank; level; grade	L.2a
170	即使	jíshǐ	even; even if	L.3b
171	几乎	jīhū	almost; nearly	L.8a
172	记得	jìdé	to remember; to recall	L.7a
173	既然	jìrán	since; given the fact that	L.5a
174	夹菜	jiā cài	to pick up food with chopsticks	L.5a
175	价格	jiàgé	price	L.6a
176	价钱	jiàqián	price	L.6b
177	价值	jiàzhí	value	L.1a
178	兼并	jiānbìng	to merge; to annex; merger	L.7b
179	检验	jiǎnyàn	inspection; to inspect	L.7a
180	建立	jiànlì	to establish; to build	L.4b
181	建议	jiànyì	suggestion; to suggest	L.6a

182	健身房	jiànshēnfáng	gym	L.2a
183	降低	jiàngdī	to reduce; to lower; to cut down	L.7a
184	降价	jiàng jià	to lower prices	L.8a
185	交换	jiāohuàn	to exchange; to swap	L.3b
186	交货	jiāo huò	to deliver goods	L.7a
187	交流	jiāoliú	to exchange (ideas/information/etc.)	L.8b
188	交朋友	jiāo péngyou	to make friends	L.1b
189	交税	jiāo shuì	to pay taxes/customs duties	L.1a
190	交通	jiāotōng	traffic; transportation; communications	L.4b
191	交易	jiāoyì	deal; trade; transaction; to deal; to trade	L.4a
192	交易会	jiāoyìhuì	trade fair	L.4a
193	叫醒	jiàoxǐng	to wake sb. up (For instance: 叫醒服务 wake-up call)	L.2a
194	接待	jiēdài	to receive/admit a guest	L.4b
195	接待单位	jiēdài dānwèi	host organization	L.4b
196	接风	jiēfēng	to give a welcome reception for visitors from afar	L.5a
197	接受	jiēshòu	to accept	L.8a
198	今后	jīnhòu	from now on; henceforth; in the future	L.3b
199	紧张	jǐnzhāng	nervous; tense	L.1b
200	锦江饭店	Jǐnjiāng Fàndiàn	Jinjiang Hotel	L.2b
201	进出口	jìnchūkǒu	import and export	L.1a
202	进货	jìn huò	to purchase merchandise; to replenish stocks	L.8a
203	进口	jìnkǒu	import; to import; entrance	L.1a
204	进入	jìnrù	to enter; to get into	L.7b
205	竞争	jìngzhēng	competition; to compete	L.6b
206	竞争力	jìngzhēnglì	competitiveness	L.8a
207	敬	jìng	to offer politely	L.5a
208	久仰	jiǔyǎng	a short form of "久仰大名" which means "I have heard your illustrious name for a long time."	L.3b
209	酒店	jiǔdiàn	hotel; wine shop	L.1a
210	局长	júzhǎng	director (of a government office or bureau)	L.5a
211	举行	jǔxíng	to hold (a meeting, etc.)	L.5a
212	具体	jùtǐ	specific; particular; concrete	L.3a

| 213 | 据说 | jùshuō | it is said... | L.5b |

K

214	卡	kǎ	card	L.1a
215	卡通	kǎtōng	cartoon	L.7a
216	开放	kāifàng	to open (to trade/to the public/etc.); to lift a ban or restriction	L.6b
217	考察	kǎochá	make on-the-spot investigation; observe and study	L.3a
218	考虑	kǎolǜ	to consider; to think over	L.8a
219	科技	kējì	science and technology	L.4a
220	可爱	kě'ài	cute; lovable	L.7a
221	客户	kèhù	client; customer	L.6a
222	客人	kèrén	guest; visitor	L.2a
223	客套	kètào	polite formula; civilities	L.3b
224	孔子	Kǒngzǐ	Confucius	L.5a
225	恐怕	kǒngpà	I am afraid; perhaps	L.8a
226	夸张	kuāzhāng	to exaggerate; exaggeration	L.8b
227	筷子	kuàizi	chopsticks	L.5a
228	款	kuǎn	a measure word for the design of certain things (especially clothing); item/clause (in document)	L.6a
229	亏损	kuīsǔn	financial loss; deficit; to suffer a loss	L.7b

L

230	老板	lǎobǎn	boss	L.1a
231	老话	lǎohuà	old saying; adage	L.6b
232	老一辈	lǎoyíbèi	older generation	L.5b
233	乐意	lèyì	to be willing/happy to	L.1b
234	类型	lèixíng	type; category	L.7b
235	冷盘	lěngpán	cold dish; hors d'oeuvres	L.5a
236	礼貌	lǐmào	courtesy; politeness	L.3b
237	礼品部	lǐpǐnbù	gift shop	L.2a
238	礼仪	lǐyí	etiquette; rite; protocol	L.3b
239	李信文	Lǐ Xìnwén	*a name*	L.1a
240	理解	lǐjiě	to understand	L.8b

241	利润	lìrùn	profit;	L.8a
242	良好	liánghǎo	good; well	L.2a
243	列	liè	to list	L.3b
244	零售价	língshòujià	retail price	L.6a
245	领导	lǐngdǎo	leader; leadership	L.5a
246	另外	lìngwài	in addition; besides	L.4a
247	另议	lìngyì	be discussed/negotiated separately	L.6a
248	旅馆	lǚguǎn	hotel	L.2b
249	旅行社	lǚxíngshè	travel agency	L.2b
250	旅客	lǚkè	hotel guest; traveler; passenger	L.2a

M

251	买卖	mǎimai	buying and selling; business	L.8b
252	买主	mǎizhǔ	buyer	L.6b
253	卖主	màizhǔ	seller; vendor	L.6b
254	满汉全席	Mǎn-Hàn Quánxí	the complete Manchu and Chinese banquet	L.5b
255	漫天要价	màntiān-yàojià	to quote an exorbitant price in anticipation of haggling	L.8b
256	茅台酒	Máotái Jiǔ	Maotai (liquor)	L.5a
257	贸易	màoyì	trade	L.1a
258	没什么	méishénme	it's nothing; it doesn't matter	L.4a
259	美国国际贸易公司	Měiguó Guójì Màoyì Gōngsī	American International Trading Company	L.1a
260	美容沙龙	měiróng shālóng	beauty salon	L.2b
261	密码	mìmǎ	password; secret code	L.2a
262	免费	miǎn fèi	to be free of charge	L.2a
263	免税	miǎn shuì	to exempt from taxation; tax-free; duty-free	L.1a
264	面对	miànduì	to face	L.5b
265	民营	mínyíng	privately-run	L.7b
266	名牌	míngpái	famous brand	L.8a
267	名片	míngpiàn	business card; name card	L.3a
268	某	mǒu	certain; some	L.8a
269	某些	mǒuxiē	certain (people/things/etc.); some	L.8a
270	目的	mùdì	purpose; objective; goal	L.3a
271	目录	mùlù	catalogue; list	L.6a

N

272	嗯	ǹg	"mmm" (express an agreement or satisfaction)	L.5a
273	耐心	nàixīn	patience; patient	
274	牛仔裤	niúzǎikù	jeans	L.6a
275	女士	nǚshì	woman; lady; Ms.; Miss	L.3a

P

276	陪	péi	to accompany; to keep sb. company	L.5a
277	赔本	péi běn	to sustain losses in business	L.8a
278	批	pī	a measure word for goods; batch; lot;	L.7a
279	批发价	pīfājià	wholesale price	L.6a
280	皮夹克	píjiákè	leather jacket	L.8a
281	频繁	pínfán	frequently; incessant	L.4b
282	品尝	pǐncháng	to taste; to sample	L.4a
283	品牌	pǐnpái	brand name; trademark	L.6a
284	品种	pǐnzhǒng	variety; assortment; kind	L.6b
285	葡萄酒	pútáojiǔ	wine	L.5a
286	普通	pǔtōng	ordinary; common; average	L.5b

Q

287	期间	qījiān	duration; period; time	L.3a
288	企业	qǐyè	enterprise; business	L.7b
289	洽谈	qiàtán	to talk over with; to negotiate; negotiation	L.3a
290	签订	qiāndìng	to conclude and sign (a contract, etc.)	L.3a
291	亲眼	qīnyǎn	with one's own eyes; personally	L.4a
292	轻松	qīngsōng	relaxed; light	L.1b
293	请客	qǐng kè	invite/entertain guests; treat sb. (to a meal)	L.4b
294	秋季	qiūjì	autumn	L.3a
295	取决	qǔjué	be decided by; to depend on	L.8b
296	确定	quèdìng	to define; to determine; to settle; to decide firmly	L.3a

R

297	让价	ràng jià	to better one's price	L.8a
298	热炒	rèchǎo	a fried dish (stir-fried, etc.)	L.5b
299	人民币	rénmínbì	RMB (Chinese currency)	L.2a

300	日程	rìchéng	schedule; itinerary	L.3a
301	日程表	rìchéngbiǎo	schedule; agenda; itinerary	L.4b
302	入境	rù jìng	to enter a country	L.1a
303	入口	rùkǒu	entrance	L.5b
304	入席	rù xí	to take one's seat (at a ceremony, etc.)	L.5a

S

305	善于	shànyú	be good at; be adept in	L.8b
306	商品	shāngpǐn	merchandise; goods; commodity	L.4a
307	商务	shāngwù	business, business affairs	L.2a
308	商务中心	shāngwù zhōngxīn	business center	L.2a
309	商业	shāngyè	commerce; trade; business	L.1a
310	商业价值	shāngyè jiàzhí	commercial value	L.1a
311	上菜	shàng cài	to serve (food); to place dishes on the table	L.5a
312	上当	shàng dàng	to be fooled/taken in	L.6b
313	上网	shàng wǎng	to access the internet	L.2a
314	上座	shàngzuò	the seat of honor	L.5a
315	稍	shāo	a little; a bit; slightly	L.3a
316	稍后	shāohòu	later	L.3a
317	少不了	shǎobuliǎo	cannot do without; indispensable	L.4b
318	设备	shèbèi	equipment; facilities	L.7a
319	设计	shèjì	design; to design	L.6a
320	设施	shèshī	facilities; amenities	L.2a
321	设有	shèyǒu	to have; to include within	L.2b
322	申报	shēnbào	declaration; to declare (dutiable goods)	L.1a
323	申报单	shēnbàodān	declaration form	L.1a
324	深刻	shēnkè	deep; profound	L.7a
325	深圳	Shēnzhèn	*a city name*	L.3a
326	甚至	shènzhì	even (to the extent that ...); to go so far as	L.4b
327	生产区	shēngchǎnqū	production area	L.7a
328	生产效率	shēngchǎn xiàolǜ	productivity	L.7a
329	生意	shēngyi	business; trade	L.1a
330	圣诞节	Shèngdàn Jié	Christmas	L.7a
331	失败	shībài	to fail; failure	L.8a

332	时差	shíchā	time difference; jet lag	L.5a
333	实行	shíxíng	to implement; to put into practice; to carry out	L.6b
334	史强生	Shǐ Qiángshēng	*a name*	L.1a
335	使	shǐ	to make; to cause	L.1b
336	使用	shǐyòng	to use	L.2b
337	世界五百强（企业）	Shìjiè Wǔbǎi Qiáng (qǐyè)	Fortune Global 500 (companies)	L.7b
338	市场	shìchǎng	market	L.6a
339	市场价	shìchǎngjià	market price	L.6a
340	市场经济	shìchǎng jīngjì	market economy; market-directed economy	L.6b
341	式样	shìyàng	style	L.6a
342	事先	shìxiān	in advance; beforehand	L.4b
343	试生产	shìshēngchǎn	to manufacture on a trial basis; trial production	L.6a
344	试销品	shìxiāopǐn	trial item/products	L.6a
345	视频	shìpín	video	L.6a
346	适当	shìdàng	proper(ly)	L.8a
347	手续	shǒuxù	procedure; formalities	L.1a
348	首先	shǒuxiān	in the first place; first of all	L.3b
349	数量	shùliàng	quantity	L.8a
350	刷卡	shuā kǎ	to swipe a card; to use a credit card	L.2a
351	双方	shuāngfāng	both sides/parties (in negotiations, etc.)	L.3a
352	顺便	shùnbiàn	conveniently	L.3b
353	顺便说一句	shùnbiàn shuō yí jù	by the way; incidentally	L.3b
354	顺利	shùnlì	smooth(ly)	L.1a
355	说法	shuōfǎ	way of saying sth.; wording	L.8b
356	私人	sīrén	private; personal	L.4b
357	私有	sīyǒu	privately-owned	L.7b
358	随便	suíbiàn	as you like; do as one pleases	L.5a
359	随时	suíshí	at any time	L.3a
360	孙子兵法	Sūnzǐ Bīngfǎ	*The Art of War* by Sun Wu, ancient Chinese philosopher during the Chunqiu period (777- 476 B.C.).	L.6b

T

361	台湾	Táiwān	Taiwan	L.1a

362	谈判	tánpàn	negotiations; talks; to negotiate	L.1b
363	讨价还价	tǎojià-huánjià	to bargain; to haggle	L.8b
364	套房	tàofáng	suite	L.2a
365	特价	tèjià	special/bargain price	L.8a
366	特色菜	tèsècài	special dish; chef's special	L.5a
367	提出（来）	tí chū (lái)	to pose (questions); to raise (an issue); to put forward (one's opinion);	L.7a
368	提供	tígōng	to provide; to supply; to offer	L.2b
369	甜点	tiándiǎn	dessert	L.5b
370	填	tián	to fill out	L.1a
371	挑战	tiǎozhàn	challenge; to challenge	L.6b
372	调整	tiáozhěng	to adjust	L.7b
373	听起来	tīng qǐlái	to sound like; to sound as if	L.4a
374	通常	tōngcháng	normal(ly); usual(ly)	L.2b
375	同类	tónglèi	the same kind; similar	L.6a
376	头衔	tóuxián	official title	L.3b
377	投放	tóufàng	to throw in; to put (sth. on the market)	L.7a
378	投资	tóuzī	to invest; investment	L.3a
379	投资环境	tóuzī huánjìng	investment environment	L.3a
380	推出	tuīchū	to present (to the public); to put out	L.6a
381	推动	tuīdòng	to push forward; to promote; to give impetus to; to spur	L.7b

W

382	哇	wa	wow; (expresses surprise)	L.2a
383	外币	wàibì	foreign currency	L.2a
384	外币兑换	wàibì duìhuàn	foreign currency exchange	L.2a
385	外贸局	wàimàojú	Foreign Trade Bureau	L.5a
386	外资	wàizī	foreign investment	L.7b
387	外资企业	wàizī qǐyè	foreign-capital enterprises	L.7b
388	完备	wánbèi	well provided; complete with everything	L.2a
389	玩具	wánjù	toy	L.4a
390	王府井希尔顿酒店	Wángfǔjǐng Xī'ěrdùn Jiǔdiàn	Hilton Beijing Wangfujing Hotel	L.2b
391	王国安	Wáng Guó'ān	*a name*	L.3a

392	王总	Wáng zǒng	a short form for President Wang	L.3a
393	微笑	wēixiào	to smile; smile	L.1b
394	闻名	wénmíng	famous; well-known	L.5b
395	问候	wènhòu	greeting	L.3a
396	无论	wúlùn	no matter; regardless	L.4b
397	五星级	wǔxīngjí	five star ranking; five star	L.2a

X

398	西装	xīzhuāng	Western-style clothes; suit	L.6a
399	吸引	xīyǐn	to attract; to draw	L.6a
400	吸引力	xīyǐnlì	appeal	L.6a
401	洗衣袋	xǐyīdài	laundry bag	L.2a
402	洗衣房	xǐyīfáng	laundry room	L.2a
403	细心	xìxīn	carefulness; thoroughness; careful(ly); thorough(ly)	L.8b
403	先进	xiānjìn	advanced; state-of-the-art	L.7a
405	现金	xiànjīn	cash	L.2a
406	箱子	xiāngzi	suitcase; box	L.1a
407	想不到	xiǎngbudào	unexpected	L.4b
408	销路	xiāolù	sales; market	L.8a
409	销售	xiāoshòu	sales; marketing; to sell; to market	L.7b
410	效率	xiàolǜ	efficiency	L.7a
411	效益	xiàoyì	beneficial result; benefit	L.7b
412	信息	xìnxī	information	L.6b
413	信用卡	xìnyòngkǎ	credit card	L.2a
414	兴趣	xìngqù	interest; hobby	L.6a
415	行李	xíngli	luggage; baggage	L.1a
416	幸会	xìnghuì	to be honored to meet (sb.)	L.3a
417	姓名	xìngmíng	full name	L.3b
418	修改	xiūgǎi	to revise; to modify; revision	L.4a
419	选择	xuǎnzé	choice; to choose	L.6b
420	寻求	xúnqiú	to seek; to pursue	L.7b
421	询问	xúnwèn	to ask about; to inquire	L.6a
422	迅速	xùnsù	rapid; speedy; prompt	L.4a

Y

423	押金	yājīn	deposit; cash pledge	L.2a

424	亚洲	Yàzhōu	Asia	L.3a
425	严肃	yánsù	serious; solemn; stern	L.1b
426	邀请	yāoqǐng	to invite; invitation	L.4a
427	业务	yèwù	business; professional work	L.4a
428	一般	yìbān	general(ly); common(ly)	L.2b
429	一般来说	yìbān láishuō	generally speaking	L.2b
430	一方面	yì fāngmiàn	one side; on the one hand	L.6b
431	一口气	yìkǒuqì	in one breath; at one go; without a break; in one stretch	L.5b
432	一言为定	yìyán-wéidìng	that's settled then	L.8a
433	遗憾	yíhàn	regrettable; to regret; to feel sorry	L.8a
434	以上	yǐshàng	over...; above...; more than	L.8a
435	引进	yǐnjìn	to introduce from elsewhere; to import	L.7a
436	印象	yìnxiàng	impression	L.7a
437	拥抱	yōngbào	to hug; to embrace	L.3b
438	优势	yōushì	advantage; superiority; dominant position	L.7b
439	尤其	yóuqí	especially	L.2b
440	由	yóu	by; through; via; from	L.6a
441	邮件	yóujiàn	mail; email	L.2a
442	游览	yóulǎn	tour; to tour; to go sight-seeing	L.2b
443	有关	yǒuguān	concerning; related to; to relate; have sth. to do with	L.6b
444	有力	yǒulì	strong; powerful	L.7b
445	有朋自远方来，不亦乐乎	yǒu péng zì yuǎnfāng lái, bú yì lè hū	Isn't it a joy to have friends coming from distant places?	L.5a
446	有助于	yǒuzhùyú	be conductive/helpful to	L.4b
447	预订	yùdìng	to reserve; to book	L.2a
448	预祝	yùzhù	to congratulate beforehand	L.5a
449	原料	yuánliào	raw material	L.7b
450	圆满	yuánmǎn	satisfactory; satisfactorily	L.5a
451	越来越	yuèláiyuè	more and more	L.1b
452	运费	yùnfèi	transport fees; freight charge	L.8a

Z

453	仔细	zǐxì	careful(ly); attentive(ly)	L.6a

454	展示	zhǎnshì	to reveal; to show; to display; to exhibit sth.	L.6a
455	张红	Zhāng Hóng	a name	L.3a
456	招待	zhāodài	to receive/entertain (guests); reception	L.5a
457	招手	zhāo shǒu	to wave (the hands); to beckon	L.1a
458	折扣	zhékòu	discount	L.8a
459	真诚	zhēnchéng	sincerity; sincere	L.5b
460	正式	zhèngshì	formal(ly); official(ly)	L.3a
461	政策	zhèngcè	policy	L.6b
462	政府	zhèngfǔ	government	L.7b
463	之一	zhīyī	one of ...	L.5a
464	支持	zhīchí	support; to support	L.7b
465	只有	zhǐyǒu	only	L.6b
466	知己知彼	zhījǐ-zhībǐ	to know one's self and know the enemy	L.6b
467	知名度	zhīmíngdù	name recognition; reputation	L.8a
468	指教	zhǐjiào	to give advice/comments	L.3a
469	制度	zhìdù	system	L.8b
470	制造	zhìzào	to make; to manufacture	L.7a
471	质量	zhìliàng	quality	L.6a
472	中心	zhōngxīn	center	L.2a
473	中央	zhōngyāng	central (government, etc.)	L.7b
474	周到	zhōudào	attentive; considerate; thorough	L.3a
475	逐渐	zhújiàn	gradually	L.7b
476	主管	zhǔguǎn	person in charge; to be in charge of	L.3a
477	主人	zhǔrén	host; master	L.4b
478	主任	zhǔrèn	director	L.3a
479	助理	zhùlǐ	assistant	L.3a
480	著名	zhùmíng	famous; celebrated	L.4a
481	专门	zhuānmén	specially; special; specialized	L.4a
482	资金	zījīn	financial resources; funds	L.7b
483	资料	zīliào	date; means; material	L.6a
484	自从	zìcóng	since	L.6b
485	自然	zìrán	of course; naturally	L.5b
486	自我	zìwǒ	self; oneself	L.7a

487	自助	zìzhù	self-help; self-serving	L.2a
488	总裁	zǒngcái	chief executive officer; CEO	L.3a
489	总经理	zǒngjīnglǐ	president; general manager	L.1a
490	总算	zǒngsuàn	finally; at last	L.1a
491	租车	zū chē	to rent a car; car rental	L.2b
492	租赁	zūlìn	to rent; to lease; lease	L.7b
493	组装	zǔzhuāng	to assemble; assembly	L.7a
494	组装线	zǔzhuāngxiàn	assembly line	L.7a
495	最好	zuìhǎo	best; had better; it would be best	L.2b
496	醉	zuì	drunk	L.5b
497	左右	zuǒyòu	about; around	L.4a
498	座位	zuòwèi	seat	L.5b

句型表（上册）
The List of Sentence Patterns (Volume I)

A

001	A 对 B 有影响		A has an impact on B; A influences B	L.7b
002	A 分为（/成）……		A can be categorized into...	L.7b
003	A 比 B + Adj. + rough estimation (or specific quantity)		A is + rough estimation (or specific quantity) + Adj. than B	L.2a
004	A 比 B + V. + specific quantity (or rough estimation)		A V. + specific quantity (or rough estimation) than B	L.7a
005	A 不比 B + Adj.		A is not more Adj. than B (namely, A and B are about same)	L.8a
006	A 代表 B + V. ……		A + V. ... on behalf of B	L.3a
007	A 给 B……的印象 /A 给 B 的印象 + Adj.		A makes ... impression on B	L.7a
008	A 为 B + V. + sth.		A V. sth. for B	L.2a
009	A 也好，B 也好		no matter whether A or B	L.7b
010	A 有助于 B		A is conducive/helpful to B	L.4b
011	按照……		according to; on the basis of	L.6a

B

012	……，便于……		(do sth. which would make) easy to; convenient for...	L.3b
013	把 Obj. 一口气 V. + Complement		do sth. at one go/at a stretch	L.5b
014	把 sth. V. 成……		V. sth. to/into/as...	L.4a
015	不但……而且……		not only...but also...	L.2a
016	不得不		have no choice but to; have to	L.8a
017	不仅……而且……		not only ... but also...	L.4b

C

018	除了……以外，还……		besides/in addition to..., also...	L.4a

D

019	当……的时候		when...	L.1b
020	对……感兴趣		to be interested in...	L.6a

| 021 | 对……满意 | be satisfied with… | L.7a |

F

| 022 | 反正 | anyway; anyhow; in any case | L.4a |
| 023 | 非……不可 | (absolutely) must… | L.8b |

G

024	赶在……前 V.	rush/hurry to V. before …	L.7a
025	跟……有关系	have something to do with…; related to …	L.6a
026	固然……不过……	it is true that … but …	L.8b

J

027	即使……还是……	even (if) … still …	L.8a
028	即使……也……	even (if) … (still/also) …	L.3b
029	既……又……	both A and B; A as well as B	L.3b
030	既然……就……	given the fact that/since … then …	L.5a
031	就	(an adverb, serves as an emphatic marker; it is usually stressed in speaking)	L.1a
032	就……进行（/举行）谈判（/会谈/洽谈）	have negotiations (talk) on …	L.8a
033	就是……也……	even (if)…	L.5b
034	据说……	it is said …; according to (sb./media) said	L.5b

K

| 035 | 可 + Adj. + 了 | (可 is an emphatic adverb) | L.2a |

L

| 036 | 连……都/也…… | even/including… | L.4a |

M

| 037 | （sb. V.……的）目的是…… | the purpose (that sb. V. …) is … | L.3a |

N

| 038 | 能 + V. + 多少 + 就 + V. + 多少 | to V. as much/many as one can | L.1b |

Q

039	请 A 帮 B + V.……	ask A to help B to do …	L.2b
040	取决于……	be decided by …; depend on …	L.8b

R

041	让 sb.（来）V.……	let sb. V./allow sb. to V. (usually provide some sort of service)	L.3a
042	如果……（的话），就……	If…, then …	L.2a

S

043	善于……	be good at …	L.8b
044	使 / 让	to make; to cause	L.1b
045	是来 / 去……的	(express purpose in coming or going)	L.1a
046	虽然……但是 / 可是……	although … but/however …	L.5a

T

047	提起……	to mention …; to speak of …	L.1a

W

048	无论……还是……，（……）都……	no matter … or …	L.4b

X

049	习惯 + V.	be used to/accustomed to V.	L.3b
050	先……，再……，最后……	first … , then …, lastly …	L.5b
051	像……等等	such as …etc.	L.2b
052	谢谢 + clause	thank + clause	L.1a

Y

053	一方面……，一方面……	on the one hand…, on the other hand…; for one thing…, for another…	L.6b
054	一是……，二是……	one (of the reasons, etc.) is…, the other is…; on the one hand…, on the other hand…	L.7a
055	由 sb.+ V.+ sth.	（由 introduces the person in charge of a given task）	L.6a
056	又……又……	both …and …	L.6b

057	……，尤其是 + N. (or nominal phrase)	..., especially + N. (or nominal phrase)	L.2b
058	……，有谁还能 / 还能不……呢？	..., what person still can / still can not...?	L.4b
059	越来越……	more and more	L.1b

Z

060	……真不错！	...is not bad; ... is very good	L.1a
061	……之一	one of ...	L.5a
062	在……过程中	in the process of ...	L.7b
063	在……期间	during (a certain period of time)	L.3a
064	在……上	in terms of ...; as far as ...	L.6b
065	这么多……（我 /sb.）都 V. 不过来了	there are so many... that one cannot V. all of them	L.5a
066	只要……，就……	as long as ... then ...	L.1b
067	只有……才……	only if... (then) ...	L.6b
068	自从……以后	(ever) since ...	L.6b
069	最好 + V.	had better do...; it would be best to do...	L.2b